The New Lonely

by

Ethan Renoe

For the nerds at FFBC
who have made a home for me in their community,
showed me how to love even when it freaking blows,
& ignited a fresh appreciation for Nicolas Cage.

May you come to know Christ more deeply,
to rest in Him
and delight in Him.

REGISTRY

FOREWORD
by Roommate Robb

I first met Ethan at our mutual friend's thirteenth birthday party. His size was age appropriate as were his braces. His hair was curly, unkempt and embroidered with a rat-tail in the back that was well out of style even in 2003. His family moved away for most of his adolescent education until they returned to the mountains of the west so Ethan could finish high school.

The next time I saw Ethan he was four years older and not much taller. His hair was the same curled greasy mop with the exception of the rat-tail. He was, all things considered, not much different from the boy I had seen at the party years earlier. I was deeply entrenched in the friend group I had established over the years at our small private school when he re-entered the community to find old friends and new acquaintances. He looked like that puzzle piece that you know is supposed to fit into the picture but no matter how hard you look you just can't find where it went. You couldn't define Ethan using the classic high school clique classifications of jock, drama kid, or even nerd.

Ethan was Ethan.

In the days leading up to our high school graduation, Ethan and I generally enjoyed one another's company but it could not be said that we were close friends. I spent most of my time adapting my own personality to that of the popular group while Ethan seemed to be off on his own adventures doing things the "Ethan way" while the rest of us were just trying to fit in somewhere.

Graduation came and passed and Ethan and I went our separate ways to live our separate lives and did not speak to each other for several years.

As fate would have it, when we were both in our mid 20's and had wandered back to that same Denver suburb, we bumped into each other at the gym one day. In appearance Ethan was nothing like the scrawny shaggy little teenager I remembered. He was bulked up and tatted out but still had the same goofy smile and charismatic laugh. As we were both staying with our parents and didn't have a lot of friends in the area we started getting coffee together regularly and something became glaringly obvious: WE SHOULD HAVE BEEN CLOSE FRIENDS FROM THE BEGINNING.

I had been so wrapped up in relationships which stopped at the surface that I was blind to the potentially significant relationships that were floating in front of my eyes. When the relationships I thought were constructive ended as quickly as they had begun, I realized I had no one I could call a best friend. It is at a time like that when a human feels most alone. Not when you are physically alone but when you feel like there is no other person who knows you.

The New Lonely is a book for those of us who know the sinking feeling of isolation you get when you're suffocating in a crowd. What this book has to teach those familiar with this feeling is that most, if not all people feel this way at some point in their lives. The population is growing faster than ever and large cities are expanding as rural America dwindles. Our society is more densely packed now than it has been throughout human history. Relationships are meant to be measured in quality not quantity. *The New Lonely* inspires its readers to pursue the relationships that have the potential for the greatest depth and the most difficult challenges. Instead of cutting the corners of your personality to fit it into the puzzle you want it to belong to, maybe it just belongs in a different picture.

-Robb Payne

PREFACE

When I began typing up the outline for this book, I began whispering to myself, *Holy Bluetooth! I'm not qualified to talk about the psychological effects of loneliness, much less the intricate structures and patterns of addiction! People study these things for years, and we're still not much closer to eliminating them from the earth!*

But there is one thing I am qualified to write about. If nothing else in the whole world, I am qualified to tell my own story and share my own experience of the world. Despite being an extrovert, I have spent many years of my life on the run. I've run from friends and family; I've avoided putting down deep roots for fear of being known. I embrace every one of the one thousand and one punk rock songs about feeling alone in a crowded room.

So it's through that lens I will be penning these non-linear thoughts on loneliness.

In the early stages of outlining and coming up with ideas for this book, I visited various high schools, churches and organizations of all sorts in order to collect—for lack of a better word—data. I wanted to see what other people were thinking about loneliness and make sure I wasn't the only one feeling these things.

Turns out I wasn't.

I'm not a scientific researcher or clinical psychologist; I'm just a poet with an observation.

Between some of the chapters, you may find a poem or piece of prose. They accidentally spilled out of me in weaker moments of passionate longing or lonely nostalgia, and I wanted to throw them in the mix just to add a little crunch to the sundae.

e

WHAT IS THE NEW LONELY?

Early in 2012, I was working for an organization in Boston when a friend called me up and asked if I wanted to help him out with an idea. It had something to do with Nigeria, evangelism, mobilizing communities, and a bunch of other enigmatic power words. I called him back a week later and told him I was in.

"Great!" he said. "You're the co-president!"

I was stunned.

Never had I been a part of starting something from nothing, much less, the co-president of a non-profit organization in Nigeria. We made a plan to meet in New York City and fly to Africa together.

The next couple weeks flew by and I decided that, rather than buy a bus or plane ticket to NYC, I would backpack it. The trip from Boston to New York in early springtime is beautiful as it cuts across Connecticut, weaving through hills just beginning to awaken into green. I stayed with some friends and some strangers along the way before finally making it to the Big Apple. I came up out of Grand Central Station into the warm day and met up with a friend who happened to be staying in the city as well and we wandered around the city until nightfall.

Early the next morning I journaled in Starbucks before going to hear one of my favorite preachers—Tim Keller—at his church on the Upper West side. I burned time by wandering around Central Park and exploring random streets and by the time darkness descended, I found myself in Chinatown.

Now, this was before smartphones spread their information like wildfires across the land, so, armed with my flip phone, I wandered through the city, hoping to stumble upon a cheap hostel for the night. I discovered that cheap hostels in NYC start around $70 a night, so I reluctantly shelled out my cash to the front desk worker and she led me up some staircases to show me my room.

The floor where I stayed was more of a huge room divided into smaller rooms by thin plywood sheets. It was also silent. I felt like there was not another living soul on the level, despite being in the middle of the biggest city in America.

She opened my room and I peeked inside, thinking *Oh, she showed me the broom closet by accident! What a funny joke!*

But this was no joke. She ushered me through the plywood door and told me to be out by 11 am, or I would be charged for another night.

I walked into the cubicle, wondering why on earth these ten square feet were worth $70 a night. There was about a two-foot gap next to the bed where I could stand, and a mattress you would get if you cut a normal mattress in half.

I read some books, pulled up a few web pages on my flip phone (two minutes to load each page), and tried to sleep.

I was alone.

I was surrounded by people. I could have left the confines of my little plywood refrigerator box and been surrounded by millions of other humans. Could have gone to a club or smoked a cigarette with an old pigeon lady. I could have worked out. I could have eaten at any one of a hundred great restaurants.

But I remained alone.

The next day I woke up minutes before 11am and bolted out of bed. I shoved everything into my backpack and shot down the stairs to avoid another $70 charge. At some point in my hasty departure, the idea came to me to visit my grandparents in Pennsylvania. I had a few more days to kill before my friend and I flew to Nigeria, and I wanted to spend them with two people I loved. I honestly have no recollection of how I found the Amtrak station (or anything, prior to the magic of iPhones, for that matter) but I hustled there and bought my ticket to Center-of-Nowhere, Pennsylvania.

My two and a half days in NYC had worn me out. The speed of the city was foreign to me back then, as was the constant noise and the endless flood of humanity. The three hour train ride was quiet though, and as we sped across the tracks, the intense busyness of New York gave way to the lush green serenity of farm country.

I left over eight million humans to be with two.

If human beings primarily relied on math to make decisions, then my choice would be considered absurd. Loneliness would be cured by being near *more* people, not less. Lonely people would flock *to* the city instead of leaving it.

Because eight million is a higher number than two.

But people are not mathematical beings, or at least I'm not, and more people does not equate to less loneliness.

I fled to the comfort of my grandparents' home because they love me.

They know me. There is instant acceptance and connection when I see my family. Even if they are surrounded by miles of cornfields, the two of them make me feel less lonely than a million New Yorkers.

And this, in essence, is the New Lonely.

We are a people more connected than ever before. We have instant access to millions of people via the World Wide Web and our social networks. We can pick up a phone and make a call to the other side of the country or Skype a friend in Peru. The resounding chorus of our age is one about being alone in a crowded room.

We are the backpacker in New York City: Connected to scores of people, but lonelier than a passing cloud.

The New Lonely is a paradox. It's why the wanderer in New York is lonelier than the grandson in Pennsylvania. It's why the 21-year-old model with 40,000 followers is lonelier than the small town girl with two best friends.

In the past, one was lonely because he had no people around him. Or maybe she was the weird girl at school and no one ever talked to her. They were the Classical Lonely. They were lonely because there were no other people for them to connect with.

Today, I think we are lonely for a different reason. There is no shortness of people for us to connect with—just try to find someone on Facebook with under 100 friends. There is a social club, website, and online group for every conceivable interest, all united by the Internet. The nerds are no longer the social outcasts.

But this is not one of those books aimed at simply guilting you offline and away from social media.

The overall problem for The New Lonely is not quantity, but *quality*. We often sacrifice the depth of our relationships for a greater number of connections. Honestly, how deep are your relationships?

A bigger network.

A larger following.

A greater platform.

Today we are not lonely because we lack people, but because we lack depth. We lack intimacy with those we call our friends, family, and significant others. We lack the willpower to focus our attention on one person, face-to-face, on a regular basis.

Additionally, we are more distant from ourselves. We fear silence and isolation. The person in the mirror is more of a stranger than someone we know well and are comfortable living inside. We're distracted and off-center.

You feel it?

That funny feeling—that hollow, echoing ache—is the New Lonely.

When I use the word "loneliness" in this book, I'm most often referring to The New Loneliness; this modern combination of anxiety and unrest resulting in a notable lack of peace which we usually mistake for loneliness. We mistake it for loneliness because it is only revealed when we are alone and quiet. The throbbing absence of peace shows up in the silence.

Throughout the rest of this book, I will use the words 'lonely' and 'loneliness' without necessarily explaining what I mean by them. At times, the terms will refer to 'Classical Loneliness,' which describes widows, prisoners, desert island castaways and anyone else who is truly *alone* and lonely. It may describe you at times in your life, when you were cut off and friendless. Other instances, the terms will refer to this lack of peace inside many of us which is only apparent when we are alone with ourselves. Most of us try to drown out this angst with noise, distractions, and other means of escape, but it always seems to be there, lurking beneath the surface.

This book has too many personal anecdotes to be a self-help book, and too many hard-won insights to be a memoir. It is part comedy and part tragedy. I make no promises about this book as a means to escape your loneliness, nor do I vow to examine *all* causes and contributors.

But I do hope to push you to think. I hope this book will make you reconsider the way you see certain elements of our culture and how you engage with your loved ones. Technology is a big part of this, but not the only part, and I hope you'll think through many of the ways you use it. Culture is another hefty contributor, as you will see, and hopefully we'll be able to examine it objectively, noting shifts that have occurred leading to this widespread feeling of loneliness...or something like it.

If nothing else, I hope this book will be like a holey old blanket. You can wrap it around the cold limbs of your mind when the wintery feelings roll in and hopefully, it will be of some comfort. Perhaps there will also be consolation, realizing you're not the only one thinking and feeling this way.

And maybe, just maybe, you'll begin to dive beneath the surface of our culture's superficial values and escape the ranks of the New Lonely.

THE PAIN

"I'm just looking for someone who speaks the same language as me."
-Leaving Weather

The winters on Cape Cod are a unique kind of beautiful.

Gray.

Everything is gray.

The trees have shed all their leaves and the trunks remain naked and cold, playing dead amidst the passing New Englanders.

You could stand beside the ocean and watch the dark gray waves crash against the rocky beaches and sing the same song it's been singing for a thousand years. Martha's Vineyard and Nantucket rest on the horizon, or just beyond it, depending on where you are on the cape. Black rocks stretch out into the water in jetties as barnacles and mussels cling to them for safety from the strength of the tide. The sand is frozen into hard sheets so you can walk atop it for the most part, occasionally crunching down through the surface.

The marshes and bays are full of dead reeds, laid flat against their rimy beds. For a few months, the peninsula seems quiet. White brume escapes your mouth as you whisper to your mates about the coming storm. Or perhaps you're only whispering to yourself, since the population of the Cape triples in the summertime, but for now you're alone.

Winters are different, even alien, from the vibrant summers on Cape Cod when the trees are green, the ocean is warm, and lovesick teenagers drop from rope swings into any of her 365 ponds. But winter is quiet, lacking the shouts and squeals of children running around in the greenery. It's as if the snow and constant cloud cover absorb most of the sounds of the environment, causing the cold months to feel muffled, even eerily silent.

I spent several winters on Cape Cod, but the one that seems to haunt my memory the most was the first after high school. I had graduated in Colorado and moved east for a girl, but our relationship didn't even survive to the end of the summer. I initially moved in with two high school friends until early in the fall, until one of them burnt down our apartment building trying to make fried Oreos. So I rented out the second floor of an elderly French lady's home in Hyannisport, near the Kennedy Compound. I spent the majority of my first year of college alone.

I lived alone.

I went to school alone.

I bought groceries alone.

I worked out alone.

For some reason, the most jarring display of my isolation was when I would drive from place to place. Maybe this was because these were the times I was unable to be distracted by schoolwork, television and movies. I owned a bright red Volkswagen, a stark contrast to the bleak surroundings, and as I piloted her from place to place, I remember this intense longing for companionship. I wanted so badly for someone to be riding shotgun with me. The desire was so strong it nearly felt like the pain was physical—the aching in my bones welled up inside me and was unbearable.

So I did what most of us do when the pain becomes too big to handle head-on: I escaped. I perfected the art of film snobbery, sometimes watching three films a day on that second floor in Hyannisport. I favored independent or foreign films, hoping their ambiguity would help me appear more intellectual before my sea of invisible friends.

I also escaped into daydreams of adventure. I pictured myself wandering the world, sailing under the southern tip of Cape Horn and earning the golden hoop earring sailors could only wear if they had survived that treacherous voyage. I read endless travel blogs and adventure journals, hoping one day my time would come and I could up and leave the gray silence of the Cape in exchange for an adrenaline-fueled life abroad. It would only be a few months later I would be boarding a plane in Los Angeles heading to Fiji on my first stint abroad with YWAM.

But we're not there yet.

We're still in that place between the barren oaks. In my car, cutting through the miles of ashen branches on either side, indefinitely alone and feeling empty. Sometimes I wonder if those arid places within us will ever be quenched; if the wintry feelings that haunt us at our core will ever give way to a season of springtime.

This is a true place to be.

Don't think for a second that because I've written a book on loneliness the forsaken feelings don't arise when the sun slips below the horizon and my friends are preoccupied. Even now, I'm realizing that by agreeing to author another book, I have sacrificed a slice of my life as an offering to the gods of loneliness. You don't write a book while surrounded by friends.

Loneliness hurts. Donald Miller sums it up well in his blockbuster *Blue Like Jazz,* 'If loving other people is a bit of heaven then certainly isolation is a bit of hell."

Rich Mullins, the great singer/songwriter of the 90's, once offered a somber take on his bouts with loneliness in an interview:

> "I would always be frustrated with relationships even when I was engaged. I had a ten-year thing with this girl and I would often wonder why, even in those most intimate moments of our relationship, I would still feel really lonely. And it was just a few years ago that I finally realized that friendship is not a remedy for loneliness. Loneliness is a part of our experience and if we are looking for relief from loneliness in friendship, we are only going to frustrate the friendship. Friendship, camaraderie, intimacy, all those things and loneliness live together in the same experience..."

Loneliness is a part of our experience; a part of our humanity.

It is normal to be lonely.

Yet I read that and to some degree become slightly deflated. It's a rather hopeless outlook from one of the fathers of contemporary Christian music, right? I wonder if loneliness is something we should not see as evil, but rather as a means to something else. After all, we must believe that if Jesus—by way of becoming human—understands everything we experience in this lifetime, He also experienced loneliness. Brand New asked Him this question in their aptly titled song *Jesus Christ,*

> "Well Jesus Christ, I'm alone again
> So what did you do those three days you were dead?
> 'cause this problem's gonna last more than the weekend."

As He hangs on the cross on Golgotha, we even see Jesus cry out, quoting the words of the psalmist, "My God, my God, why have you forsaken me?" Not only did He experience rejection from all of his disciples and friends, but even His Father, from whom He had never felt distant in all of eternity past.

If the Son of God cannot even escape feelings of loneliness, why should we hope to do any better?

To some degree, I wonder if we can't.

I wonder if there is no real and final cure to loneliness, and as Mullins pointed out, we are trapped in a somewhat lonely existence for the duration of our lives until we pass on to the next life and experience either the heights of intimacy or the ultimate depth of abandonment. Of all the surveys I performed on the subject of loneliness, there was not a single person who reported *never* feeling lonely. The surveys gave the options for feeling lonely several times a day, several times a week, a month, and never.

Not once did I receive a survey from someone who felt lonely less than several times a month.

What I do know for sure is that our means of escape and our methods of coping do nothing to ease our lonely feelings and fill the gaps we feel inside. Far too often, we are unaware of how these distractions make the problem even worse. We are a lonely people who turn to impersonal things like computer screens, music-filled earbuds and whimsical novels to try to feel less alone.

Ironic, right?

Part of the struggle of the New Lonely is getting trapped in the cyclical whirlwind our culture makes look so appealing. What I mean is, we fall prey to the fashion advertisements, and buy the latest clothes, only to feel insecure once again when those threads have fallen from popularity and newer trends have taken over. Or perhaps we will fall into a pornography addiction, turning to it when we feel too lonely to stand up, only to feel even more ashamed and unworthy of love after each episode.

There are also less nefarious-seeming escapes such as Netflix binges and aimless hours spent scrolling through social media. None of these things are inherently bad, but when they become crutches and means of escape from the tedium of our lonesome lives, they only pour gasoline on the problem. We feel lonely so we turn on an episode of our favorite sitcom. Six episodes later, we have not only made no work toward building healthy relationships in our lives, but we may now be slightly depressed because our lives and romances look nothing like those of the fictional characters we just envied for two hours.

Perhaps it's the non-fictional characters in our own lives that stir us to envy and despair. We sign into Instagram (or any other *social* network) and scroll through dozens or hundreds of posts from people who—we are convinced—all have better lives than us. So our solo night at home turns from a relaxing evening into a jealousy-fueled spiral into more loneliness and despondency.

It's a cycle. One that far too many people ever realize they are in.

Cornelius Plantinga Jr. notes in his book *Not the Way It's Supposed to Be: A Breviary of Sin:* "People feel walled in by loneliness. Whether homesick or obsessively nostalgic or exiled or romantically forlorn or self-alienated so that they are not at home even in their own skin, lonely persons ache because they are separated."

Plantinga wrote those words in 1994, not knowing how much more true they would become, or that people in 2016 would unwittingly take measures to separate themselves.

One of my least favorite things about public transportation in any major city is that every single person is now required to wear headphones. It's almost an unwritten law—if you don't have some sort of media pumping into your head, severing you from those around you, then you are the pariah. Gone are the days of boarding a train and striking up a conversation with the interesting gentleman next to you in the tweed coat. We have replaced him with the interesting podcast or the latest track from our favorite band. We have separated ourselves.

I did a quick survey of my music library and within five minutes, came up with this list of bitter yet familiar sentiments: ·

Sometimes a crowded room can feel the most alone
-Mat Kearney, Wait

I know you're all alone in a crowd full of friends
-TobyMac, Atmosphere

I'm completely alone at a table of friends,
I feel nothing for them, I feel nothing, nothing.
-Bright Eyes, Hit the Switch

I know what it's like on a Saturday night
To be alone on a crowded street
-Jon Foreman, Resurrect Me

There's something about our generation that feels so removed from those around us. There is a reason this is a recurring theme in the songs we listen to, and I wonder if we have done it to ourselves. We feel alone in crowded rooms because we have cut ourselves off. Whether physically, with headphones blocking our ears, or emotionally as insecurities drive us to hide when in public. What better way to hide than behind the masks we've constructed for ourselves?

I'll be the first to raise my hand in familiarity with the lyrics from those songs. I can remember one time in particular in Chicago, I was invited to a house party up north near Loyola. I knew the Loyola crew were very hip and fashionable, so I carefully selected my outfit and made sure to wear it *just so* (The key is to look like you don't care how you look). There were a few friends of mine going, so we met near the train station and shot up the Red Line.

When we arrived at the house, music was playing and food and drinks were all set out for us. As the night progressed, dancing began and then stopped. And then started back up again. Then came the time when the slow songs came on and the 30 or so people in the apartment seemed to magnetize to their intended other. They whispered small jokes into the others' ear while swirled up on the hardwood floor. The single people seemed to congregate with the men standing in small circles having rich conversations, and the ladies doing likewise.

It seemed like everyone had found their place in the puzzle except me, who ended up sitting alone against a wall somewhere, wishing so badly I had someone near me to whisper little thoughts to. I was alone in a crowded room and blah blah blah...

But looking back, it was entirely my fault.

I had dressed up as someone else, attempting to look cooler than I actually was. Not only did I try to look better than I was, but I made myself seem more sophisticated through conversation, or told cool traveling stories to impress someone. I was pretending to be someone who didn't exist. If you've never tried it, it's very difficult to carry on a conversation with someone who doesn't exist.

Insecurity had driven me to look and act cooler than I was. I was unfamiliar with myself as a person, and therefore felt unable to impress anyone except by inflating and exaggerating elements of who I was. And that's why I sat alone on the floor when the slow songs began.

It's easy to shift the blame for our loneliness to others, but in reality, most of us, the New Lonely, have only ourselves to hold responsible. We create our own rhythms which lead to loneliness, and the cycle tends to hit repeat and before we know it, we don't know ourselves, we're distant from others, and we feel very, very lonely.

Loneliness is a unique animal. If it were easily solved by an increase in human contact or some miracle from the heavens, none of you would be reading this book. It comes with no guarantee that by the time you hit the back cover, you'll be free of this weight that seems to follow you around.

There is a certain ache of loneliness, and I see this feeling morphing throughout the generations, and even from person to person. Maybe you'll end up like Rich Mullins, coming to terms with the fact that loneliness will be an ongoing presence throughout your whole life, and in that realization will come a sense of peace and closure. Perhaps you will finish this book and realize areas in your life where you have been the one perpetuating your own cycles of loneliness, and take steps to disrupt the perennial sorrow.

Whatever the outcome, I hope that in reading these words, you will find that in being lonely, you are not alone. We all know well the misery of loneliness, and perhaps that fact alone will be of some consolation.

8/21/14

Will you ever put an end to this tangible gloom,
or am I knocking on the door of an empty room?
I came and sat down just hoping to bleed,
but the giant sits in silence with his quiet disease.
It's a tick who's always talking and he's stuck in my skin,
and I compare him to my bowels, my addiction to sin.
Will you ever lift your hand so that mine can resume,
or does the giant weep alone in an empty room?

THE STORIES WE TELL

"It's a shallow life that doesn't give a person a few scars."
— Garrison Keillor

In 2010, I was painting the side of a building in Chennai, India.

The first thing to know about Southern India is that it is hot. It's not just the "I wish I could switch from pants to shorts" kind of heat. It's the kind of heat Dante envisioned as he conjured up visions of hell. If you've ever wondered how a casserole feels as it bubbles in the oven, just go check out India. Every day when we began working, my shirt would hold up for about 20 minutes before it was completely soaked with sweat. As in,

Ethan, did you just fall into a pool? No? Oh, it's just sweat? Ok, I'm gonna go bleach my eyeballs and try to forget this.

Most days, the work was much harder than simply painting the side of a building. Some of the days we ripped up the grass from the sun hardened dirt. Other days we dug ten-foot holes for outhouses by stabbing the ground with heavy iron rods and scooping out the fragments, causing white blister-bubbles to rise from our palms.

My team was working on a church building and on this particular day, I was assigned the lighter task of painting. I was partnered with a sweet

Canadian girl named Christine, and as we applied the bright blue stain to the plaster siding, we had ample time to chat. It was not long before we began sharing our life stories.

You would think someone had shot off a starter's pistol and our verbal runners launched from their starting blocks. We couldn't get the personal tales out fast enough.

Christine shared a story from when she was 5, which reminded me of something that happened to me when I was 8, which triggered her memory of that time she was in Toronto...and on it went.

We talked over each other.

Truth be told, I think I spent most of my time speaking over Christine. I was so excited to share my experience of the world and have her see me and admire me.

Because when we tell a story from our lives, we're not just recounting facts.

Obvious as it sounds, I have come to realize that everyone has a story. Everyone has sepia-toned memories that linger in their brains and form who they are. In fact, there is not a person on earth without memories and stories and experiences. Flannery O'Connor wrote, "Anybody who has survived his childhood has enough information about life to last him the rest of his days."

There is no person on earth with a shortage of stories.

We love our tales and we love to share them.

I think the human love of swapping tales is even deeper than the love of a good plot line. Since our experiences inform who we are and who we become, sharing them becomes a deeply personal act. When someone tells you a memory from when they were young—that time dad tried to scare my aunt but got tangled up in the clothesline in the backyard—they are not simply trying to entertain you; they are inviting you into their own story. They are sharing a piece of themselves with you. A piece that has influenced the person they are in some small way.

As humans, we don't simply want to exchange data; we want to be *known*. And the types of stories we tell morph and evolve the deeper a relationship becomes.

Watch as two people date and listen to the stories they tell. The first date will revolve around an exchange of details ("I went to Harvard and now I'm working as a pancake designer for IHOP"), as well as funny stories: She will tell him about the time her dad accidentally walked into the wrong bathroom at the basketball game, while he recounts the time his college roommate launched a mouse into space.

But give the relationship some time and watch how he opens up about the first time his uncle wanted to play a dirty game with him. Or the night she tells him about the first time she searched for porn online. The stories we tell end up telling a lot about us. The deeper and more intrinsic a story is to who we are as a person, the more cautious we are with it.

No story is neutral. Every time we open our mouth to relay something we did or something that happened to us, we are inviting the hearer into a part of ourselves. It's akin to saying *Come see how I was shaped. Come look at the times that formed me and made me the person I am.*

As I painted the exterior of the bright blue church in India, I was not simply passing time with Christine. I was inviting her to *know* me. I wanted her to know me and my background. I wanted her to understand my family and how they have informed the man I'm becoming.

Think about the stories in your own life.

You probably have the fun ones, the ones that you can barely get through without chopping the story between fits of laughter.

For me it's the time four of us spontaneously decided to drive from

Denver to California. The notion came to us on a Friday in January, and Saturday we were blazing West. Tressa, Kenzie, my best friend Dave and I shot across the plains of Utah as the afternoon gave way to darkness. By the time the sun came up, we were changing into shorts at a gas station in Nevada.

A few hours later, we parked in front of an apartment building in Long Beach and tried to make new friends. We met a delightful girl who welcomed us into her apartment and told us to stay as long as we liked.

The next few days were filled with wandering around Southern California and sitting on the beach. We developed one of those 'vacation rhythms' that arises when you're in the same place for a week. Every morning, our host would go to school and Dave would go out for his run (He is one of those maniacs who runs 100 miles a week and weighs the same as a banana). Tressa and Kenzie would head out to explore on their own and I would wake up slowly and revel in the silence of the morning.

The third or fourth day we were there, the morning played out accordingly. I woke up around 8 and was alone in the apartment. Shortly after I cracked open my Bible, Dave burst through the door.

And Dave was not okay.

He was hunched over like he had run to Notre Dame and back, and his eyes were wide and red. He lurched forward into the apartment like the undead, still clad only in his running shoes and skin-sucking spandex shorts.

He looked at me through his flesh hungry eyes and spat, "I'm about to pass out!"

I rose from the couch, somewhat concerned, but mostly laughing at my friend's condition, and said, "Let me get you some water!"

"No!" he growled, then looked right at me, "Food first. Sustenance."

I was trying so hard not to laugh visibly.

He spread some peanut butter on a piece of bread, then collapsed to the floor of the kitchen, nibbling tiny bites from his creation and leaning against the cupboards. He was shivering despite the California heat and could barely move. I set a glass of water next to him but he couldn't even lift it to his lips, so I helped him drink.

Eventually, he couldn't even hold himself upright so he lay down on the white linoleum. I noticed he was drifting to sleep, so I picked him up (all 95 pounds) and carried him over to the pull-out couch where he was sleeping.

When I had covered him up, I tried to take the remnant of the sandwich from his hand and when I touched it, he mumbled, "Put it back."

I put the sandwich back and a moment later Dave was fast asleep.
I texted the others to let them know what had happened, and they all

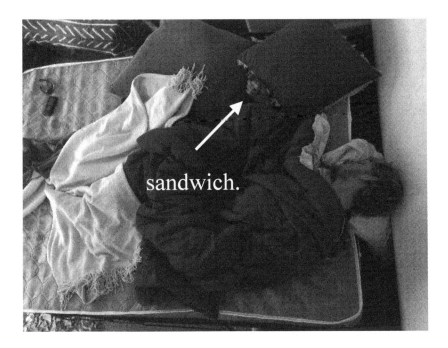

sandwich.

returned to the apartment to check on Dave. It was about an hour before our host came back. She had brought him a bottle of orange juice, thinking the glucose would help restore his system, and we decided to stir Dave from his sleep. I shook him and he slowly began moving.

Before he blinked his eyes open, he muttered, "Is there a sandwich in my hand?"

I snickered and told him yes, it's the sandwich you were so insistent on sleeping with. He sat up and we soon realized he didn't remember anything from the morning. He didn't remember finding his way back to the apartment, or bursting through the door looking like a madman. He didn't remember making a peanut butter sandwich or collapsing on the floor of the kitchen.

He remembered leaving for his run but about halfway out, it just went black. The memory never returned to him.

A few minutes later, he had finished his orange juice and began to push himself up out of bed when he paused. He was still only wearing spandex shorts and running shoes, but he had a confused look on his face, as if something was wrong.

He reached into the front of his spandex shorts and pulled out two half-melted packets of butter and held them in his palm, just staring at them.

"What are those doing in there?" he asked himself.

I was on the floor, unable to breathe from laughing.

For several minutes, he just continued his perplexed gaze at the two silvery packets of butter in his hand.

"Dave!" I managed to get out between violent sobs of laughter, "Dave, why is there butter in your shorts??"

"I...don't...know..." he said, still wondering.

The beauty of this story is that we never found out.

To this day, we have no idea why Dave ran home with butter in his spandex shorts. We don't know who put them there or why, though I have my own theories. I picture a half-crazed Zombie Dave running by one of the cafe patios in Long Beach, reaching over the small fence and grabbing a handful of silver butter packets, stashing them in his shorts as he wobbled away. Or perhaps someone saw the mostly-nude feral man and offered him a bagel and two packets of butter. He took both, putting the bagel in his mouth and the butter in his shorts.

Whatever the truth is, I don't really care because the story is better with the mysterious ending. We will never know why Dave returned to that Seal Beach apartment with two packets of butter in his spandex.

Dave and I kept the wrappers from those two packets of butter. Mine is a bookmark in my Bible to this day, a reminder of the funniest hour of my life. But it's so much more than just a silvery bookmark and a funny story.

It's a part of me. It's something I carry in my mind and relay to every new friend I meet. By hearing *The Butter Story*, they are able to see a small step on the staircase that brought me to where I am today. *The Butter Story* isn't just a yarn or a string of facts, it's a piece of me.

Nate Dimeo, in an episode of The Memory Palace entitled *Origin Stories,* describes how his family is aware of their past because of the legendary stories set in stone by their ancestors and passed down through the generations. Dimeo specifically recounts tales from a nightclub his grandfather owned, and how so much of their family's history was tied to this locale. He says,

> "They are the origin stories of one iteration of the family. My mom and her three sisters loved to hear about their mom and dad falling in love. And these stories were great. They were glamorous and dramatic. Stories from home were good, but the club stories are [great]. The Day the bear got loose, Dad's two girlfriends, The Night the Russian midgets got stuck in the snow, The Night the Great Dane danced with the stick-up man, The night my grandmother climbed up the ladder where my grandfather stood hanging the star on the Christmas tree by the coat check and surprised him with their first kiss. Or the day they piled into the backseat of the bartender's car on the way back from the beach. She sat on my grandfather's lap and he held her hand. She had never noticed her hand was so small. And she knew that she loved him. I heard that story a hundred times. The last time I was holding her hand, it was so small, while my grandfather lay dying in an adjustable bed in a Rhode Island hospital."

Just from the titles of those stories, we are drawn in and want to know more. I *badly* wish I had a story entitled "The day the bear got loose," or any of the others Nate lists. He recognized that his family's legacy shaped who he is, so much so he decided to become a storyteller by trade. To him, these are not mere myths of the past, but a big part of his person.

You'll note, however, that Nate's list of stories does not stop with the funny and romantic ones. He describes his grandparents' first kiss, but follows it up with the time he held his grandmother's small hand beside her husband's deathbed. He goes on to relay how she could no longer live in their house because of all the happy memories which haunted it.

Our lives are often a bittersweet concoction of good times mixed with the bad: the happy stories sitting on the shelf beside the tragedies. There are those stories you hold close to your chest, as if their removal may expose certain organs or a portion of your ribcage. They're the ones that really hurt to reveal.

In our efforts to be known by other people, sharing these painful parts of ourselves is necessary. Otherwise, we are only hiding behind the funny, cool, polished surfaces of a mask that hides our true personhood. Perhaps you're ashamed that you grew up in a trailer park because dad didn't have a real job, or maybe mom was an alcoholic. But these bits and pieces contribute just as much—if not more—to who we are and who we are becoming. We can choose to hide them, or to share and reveal them to those we trust.

The Navajo tribe had a unique tradition when they were making their rugs. As they were finishing the stitching, they would leave an imperfection in one of the corners where the strings would dangle out of the edge. "Because that's where the spirit enters," they say. Without imperfection, there is no access. It is our faults, weaknesses and imperfections that best connect us to others and to God.

In his book *Scary Close,* Donald Miller writes, "Grace only sticks to our imperfections. Those who can't accept their imperfections can't accept grace either." If you want to be known, *truly* known, you must risk exposure. You have to be willing to share the ugly parts as well as the pretty ones, the weaknesses alongside the strengths. This is something our generation is terrified of, and it's the reason so many of us feel alone. Only our shiny chrome exteriors can be seen in public and online, and as a result, we are not *known* in the way we long to be known.

It is a pretty isolating existence to be always seen and never known.

So that's why this book has so many stories from my life. I want to be known, to some degree, by you, the reader. But I hope this snapshot of my experience is not simply a one-way delivery from my life to yours. I hope it is an invitation for you to do the same. I hope you will pay it forward, so to speak, in becoming more vulnerable before your friends and family. I hope you learn how to tell your own stories, the comedies *and* the tragedies, building better bridges between you and those near to you.

This is an invitation to be known.

THE RAINMAKER

In 1904, Charles Hatfield moved to Los Angeles with his family. A few years prior, Hatfield had begun working on a way to conjure up clouds, and by extension, to call down rain. He had fans in the farming community who hailed him as one of the great 'rainmakers' of the day, but he insisted on describing himself as a mere "moisture accelerator."

This is a true story.

Charles Hatfield and his brother built small, simple towers about twenty to thirty feet high near farmlands that needed rain. He then lugged a special concoction of 23 chemicals in an evaporation bottle to the top of the tower, and waved it around in an effort to attract clouds.

He was very successful. Farmers would pay him and his brother $50 to build one of their towers and bring their special recipe to wave around and lure in the unsuspecting clouds in order to get rainfall on their land. Most of this was in Kansas though, and when Hatfield moved to California in 1904, he was already somewhat well known as a bringer of precipitation. His reputation grew and grew, as did the money he earned for his labor.

In 1915, the San Diego city council was preparing to throw their first world's fair, but they were worried they did not have enough water to meet the needs of the thousands of people who would come to the city as they were in the middle of a brutal drought. So the City of San Diego called Charles Hatfield, offering him $10,000 if he could attract 40 inches of rain to the Morena Dam reservoir.

Hatfield obviously took the job, but no written contract was ever drawn up; he operated purely on verbal agreement. By January 1916, he and his brother had constructed a monstrous tower beside the reservoir, producing gallons and gallons of their secret recipe.

Then they waited.

It was only a couple days before the rain began.

It rained and rained.

And it kept raining.

And it didn't stop.

Dry riverbeds filled to overflowing; farms, bridges, cables and trains were destroyed by flooding. Not one but two dams burst, causing even more damage to property.

Then the rain stopped. After fifteen days of continuous downpour, the skies dried up.

For two days.

Then the rain returned, this time worse than before, bursting a third dam and causing over twenty deaths.

In the following weeks, the city of San Diego found that the rain had caused about $3.5 million worth of damage, and they refused to pay Charles Hatfield. He protested that the city should have been more prepared before calling in a professional *moisture accelerator*, and despite the damage, he had done exactly what they had agreed upon. Hatfield tried to sue several times and ultimately, with no written contract in place, the city gave him a settlement: If he publicly admitted to causing the rain and flooding and damage, he would receive his $10,000.

Hatfield refused.

Twenty-two years passed before the city of San Diego finally declared the floods an act of God, absolving him of any wrongdoing, but also robbing him of his fee.

When I heard this story, I initially thought it was too good to be true ('Good' in the sense of what makes a great story...Not because people were killed). Then I wondered why no one has made a movie about it yet. After that, I realized how symbolic it is of our loneliness and our coping mechanisms.

The state of California was in a drought the year they hired Charles Hatfield. They were deprived of rain and moisture.

If I'm honest, most days, I feel like I'm in a drought.

I echo the sentiments of Psalm 42, as the writer compares his soul to a deer thirsting for water. I feel arid as a desert, hoping some droplets of rain will come and quench my parched soul. There are days the loneliness feels unbearable and fear takes the controls. These are the times I turn to comic books, TV shows, and more nefarious habits such as pornography or sinking into depression. Some of you may hurt yourselves or turn to other substances which promise an escape from the withering pain.

I recently did a survey at a high school in Denver and one of the questions was "What are some things you tend to do when you feel lonely?" I was floored by how many of the students claimed to turn to cutting themselves when they felt lonely. The fact that such a high percentage of high schoolers resort to such drastic means to escape their emotional pain shows just how big a problem loneliness is in our generation.

We encounter droughts like these and begin to act out of fear, but the things we turn to end up turning against us.

This theme will pop up often in this book. Think about what you tend to do when you feel lonely. We tend to turn to things that numb the pain for a while, but end up making us feel worse afterward.

Like Charles Hatfield's rain recipe, we want a magical cure to simply whip up the clouds of love and intimacy.

We are big fans of shortcuts.

We use Tinder to pair us with people we find attractive, rather than doing the harder work of getting to know another human for who they are. Other dating sites try to come off as more sophisticated, but they are all after the same thing: speeding up the process of intimacy.

Not long ago, one of the larger dating websites reached out to me and offered me a free month of their services, hoping I would meet the love of my life and in turn, publicly praise the company for their help. The first couple days were exciting. I logged in, checked out who had viewed my profile, winked at me, and showed any interest whatsoever in the digital version of Ethan Renoe.

Over time however, I realized that there was no real connection going on. In my month on the site, I chatted with a few people, but the conversations were shallow and forced, and I felt pressure to impress these girls and convince them why they should choose *me* over the other guys on the site.

Of course, like me, you probably have friends who met online or were paired up by a dating service of some sort. And that's awesome! It can be a great tool for many people. In my experience though, I felt dehumanized. I felt like I was shopping for a mate rather than letting the natural breezes of life billow.

I felt like I was trying to artificially conjure up the rain to end my personal drought.

The Slovenian philosopher Slavoj Žižek released a five minute video in 2015 entitled *Our Fear of Falling in Love* in which he describes the 'event' of falling in love. Through his characteristic snorts and twitches, he says that in the past, falling in love happened spontaneously. It was not planned.

"Let's say you stumble on the street," he says. "Somebody helps you to stand up...and of course, it's the love of your life." Žižek deconstructs this notion that modern people want the *love* without the risk of the *fall*. We want to play it safe, ensuring we don't get hurt by putting ourselves out there, but we also want to hustle things along. Which is exactly why we turn to dating services and the like in order to arrange our romantic futures.

Žižek does note that people had this in the past, only it looked like an older family member arranging a meeting or a marriage for two people, and he compares that to modern digital dating. It removes the risk. With Tinder for instance, there is a sort of guarantee that both parties have 'swiped right' and shown at least a menial amount of interest in the other before communication begins. One of the biggest obstacles to dating— initiating the first move—has suddenly been overcome.

Rather than letting our lives take their natural courses, just like the city of San Diego in 1915, we're nervous the rain won't come; that we will never meet someone who loves us for who we are, so we take measures into our own hands.

Whatever your 'moisture accelerator' of choice is, whether

drinking,

partying,

looking at porn,

Netflix,

Netflix and chill,

cutting,

escaping into books,

Snapchat/Facebook/Instagram/Twitter,

drugs,

or a plethora of others,

trying to force our way out of the drought of loneliness tends to result in more disaster than healing.

I think much of the loneliness in my life has been a refusal to be patient. I've wanted a wife, much less a girlfriend, for years. But God has been teaching me patience through failed relationships, rejections, and long periods of meeting no one new. Of course, I've tried to evade the pain of loneliness with various things. I've kissed girls despite knowing the relationship couldn't move forward. I've led girls on—both accidentally and intentionally—as a way of feeling significant or loved.

All the shortcuts we try to take only end up hurting more than helping.

Just as San Diego's government could have patiently waited for the rain to

ed to be better prepared by building water storage devices,
to put in work to cultivate intimacy in our lives. Perhaps in
eness, we should prepare ourselves to be better future
in bemoaning our current state. There is no magic wand
to make intimacy appear, just as there is (probably...) no
magic recipe to make rain fall.

Lonely people—people who are discontent in the present and always hoping for something better—tend to be *taking* people. They are people so desperate to be poured into, whenever they are with a friend, they just take from them rather than offering a friendship that is mutually beneficial. I've been that person, and chances are, you have too.

I've found that when we seek out such magic wands and maneuvers that promise to make our lives better, disaster tends to ensue. I've ruined relationships by diving too quickly into romance. I've done major damage to myself and others by pursuing pornography rather than people. There are countless 'magic wands' we could list off that have offered to help us but have done more harm than good.

One high school student demonstrated her awareness of how she uses Netflix as an escape from pain in her survey when she wrote: "When I was younger I used to hurt myself...but now I try to drown [loneliness] out with music or Netflix." As great as it is that she doesn't hurt herself anymore, I can't think Netflix is all that much better. It has become more of a numbing agent than a healing one, which only postpones addressing the roots of our loneliness.

So what lesson do we learn from Charles "The Moisture Accelerator" Hatfield?

It's important to take note of what we tend to turn to when we feel lonely. I think part of the problem is a lack of awareness of the vices disguised as harmless escapes from our pain. What do you try to use as your own 'magic wand' to draw the rain and wave the loneliness away? Take a few minutes to think about the past couple weeks or months. Pinpoint some of the times you felt lonely, hurt, or in a generally dark place. Make an inventory of things you do—both healthy and unhealthy—when you're in the throes of loneliness. Perhaps simply acknowledging and becoming aware of your 'drugs of choice' will be a good first step out of the cycle.

But I think the biggest lesson from The Rainmaker is patience.

When we can come to accept our current season of life, single, married or otherwise, and patiently wait for the winds of change to drift, I think we will be more content. I have wasted collective days of my life longing for some future bliss rather than being content as I am. As they say in Alcoholics Anonymous, the future is opaque. We are not promised a future that's better than today. What we can do is prepare ourselves to be the best person possible so that when the winds of change roll in, say, with a new relationship, we will be ready, healthy, and prepared to engage and be fruitful friends, people who can give and not just take.

People content to wait for the rain instead of trying to conjure up their own.

11/24/2014

I looked between the covers, where the lovers have their way,
but found that fleeting pleasure never did intend to stay.
I looked inside my pocket for a sum so grand and vast,
but money also robbed me, its fullness didn't last.
I looked out on the mountaintop, and by the sandy coast,
but never did I find the view that suited me the most.
I looked for Love both high and low, but never could I find
a love so deep it covered me and left my past behind.

In all my searching, I did grow to hate this empty life.
It came on me so suddenly like cattle to the knife.
But at the bottom, there I lay, exhausted from my spree;
I never had to look for it, for one day Love found me.
It came to me in silence, when the noise had wandered off,
It sounded like a whisper, coming low and sweet and soft.
My Love said He forgave me, and He made me white as snow,
for mercy conquers sacrifice and glory is my home.

BE WHEN YOU ARE

"If Wordsworth had gone back to those moments in the past, he would not have found the thing itself, but only the reminder of it; what he remembered would turn out to be itself a remembering."
-C.S. Lewis, *The Weight of Glory*

I'm sitting in a coffee shop in Denver while the stereo whispers some jazzy collaborations reminiscent of 1930's nightclubs. Women with flapper haircuts flock to the dance floor, their dresses cut dangerously short with strings swaying from the hem as their bodies swing to the plinking tunes. Each one wears gloves that rise all the way to the elbow as they smoke cigarettes through those long tubes which were so popular back then.

The men watch from the side, also dressed to the nines and sipping cocktails, exchanging stories from the war, or perhaps arguing about whether Hemingway would win in a fight against Fitzgerald. The brave men, the ones who knew what they were doing, graced the dance floor and wooed the women with their renditions of East Coast Swing or the Jitterbug.

Now a new song is on. It's a slower-paced song and a black man with a froggy voice groans over a piano as it argues with the upright bass. I picture the Jazz Age lovers dancing slowly. They are very close to each other, breathing in the other's scent. Breathing in the night. They were undistracted by the vibration of smartphones as they simply etched the night into the stone walls of their memory and two-stepped well into the morning hours.

Life was better back then.

Or at least...that's how it appears to us now.

Here in the 21st century, we get to imagine the magic of the nightclub. The women and men getting ready for the big night out; the swoosh of their feet across the hardwood floors. We picture the black and white footage of the earliest swing dancers leaping about the soundstage.

What we don't see is the next morning when they woke up with bad breath and hangovers. We don't see the hours which strung together to create days and weeks of their mundane jobs, sitting in the factory or mine. Perhaps they were accountants or dock workers. Or the homemakers, confined to a small Upper East Side flat all day, tired of living such a small life.

Maybe some of us even romanticize those elements of their lives as well, but the truth is, the times were no more rich back then than they are now. This is something referred to as a *Golden Age Myth*. The notion was first coined by Greeks and Romans, who thought people before *their* time had it better than they did. They imagined the past as a purer and better time to be alive. Keep in mind that they lived over 2,000 years ago.

Woody Allen captured this Golden Age phenomenon perfectly in his film *Midnight in Paris*. Owen Wilson plays Gil, a romantic writer engaged to an uptight, wealthy bore as they vacation in Paris. Wilson's character longs to see Paris as it was in the 1920's—especially in the rain. He wishes so badly to rewind time and relive those golden days when the city was alive and culture was erupting during the Jazz Age.

As he strolls through the streets late one night, a black old school cab rolls up and a well-dressed crew invite him in. They take him to a night club and suddenly he realizes that he is no longer in the 21st century, but has been transported back to his Golden Age. He meets Salvador Dali and Cole Porter and is interrogated by Gertrude Stein. Most curiously, he meets the enigmatic Adriana, played by French actress Marion Cotillard, and the two begin to flirt.

After several nights of returning to the Jazz Age via the mysterious black cab, Gil realizes that his muse Adriana has a Golden Age of her own. One night as they stroll about the streets of 1920's Paris, a horse-drawn carriage arrives and whisks the two of them away to the Belle Epoque of the 1890's—the era she longed to experience.

The point Allen is making is, every person since the dawn of time has been unsettled in their own time. Every single person longed for a period that was better than their own; a collective nostalgia of sorts.

"Live your own time, child," Mrs. Alvin once told the adolescent Bob Dylan, when the focus of his songs was on history instead of the present. "Sing about your own time." The young Dylan had romanticized notions about the past, but it wasn't until he recognized things happening in the world around him that his music began to influence culture.

I think we do the same thing today. I would love to visit Impressionists like Monet as he sat behind his French cottage painting lilies, or soak in the energy of the Fauves as they dashed color against their canvases. Or to hear Frank Sinatra as he banged away on the keys and crooned into one of those old-timey microphones.

More often however, I catch myself doing this with past times in my own life.

Oh, the purity of those Middle School years! When I could just listen to Relient K and hold hands with Jessica.

or,

If I could return to the yacht club on Barnstable Harbor as we swam beneath that meteor shower five thousand midnights ago, things would be good.

Things were better four, five, six, seven years ago, before everything became so complicated…

As Conor Oberst bleats in his song *Happy Birthday to Me,*

> I guess that it's typical
> To cling to memories you'll never get back again
> And to sort through old photographs
> Of a summer long ago or a friend that you used to know.

I wonder if loneliness can be a longing for a past that never really existed.

We have this reel of 8mm film our brains will play to make the past seem so alluring. The characters—our family and friends, our lovers—are permanently burnt into the spools and portrayed as flawless and romantic. As long as we fixate on this past, on this notion that our lives were so much richer and more technicolored all those years ago, the present never seems good enough.

Scientists looking into this phenomena of memory and psychology have found that when we recall The Good Old Days, we are not really remembering them at all. Instead, when we bring to mind that golden summer of 2005, we are actually remembering the last time we thought of it. The longer the time between an event and the present moment, the more times we have thought of the event, therefore, the more dreamlike and distorted the event becomes in our mind. The further removed we are from an event, the more blurry the details become as we think about it because we are not actually thinking of the event at all; we are thinking of the collection of times we have previously thought of it.

It's like looking through a tunnel to another tunnel to another tunnel that eventually leads us to the actual memory itself. Or looking at a mirror reflecting another mirror that eventually reflects the original event. It is impossible to directly recall what exactly happened, and how we felt at the time. Years later, those high school summers spent wandering the train tracks in the northeast have become locked into my mind as this flawless portrait of blissful youth because I see it *through* all the subsequent seasons between now and then. I don't see it as it truly was.

How could the present possibly compete with some beautiful projection of our lives all those years ago?

There's something I discovered during my first round of interviews with high schoolers in Colorado, and it's a simple realization: Not everyone has a past they long to return to. One freshman boy wrote in his survey, "I was almost killed by my 'father' at 6…I feel nostalgia close to never. That's the benefit of a rough childhood: Nowhere to go but up." Many of you may not fantasize about returning to the past, but possibly fall into an opposite but similar trap: Longing for the future.

The important thing is to do neither. To live in the present. To be intimate with the present moment.

I don't want to sound like one of those mystical New Age fanatics, waving about my sage incense and rubbing crystals together, but I think there is immense value in being aware of the present. God did not place you in the Jazz Age. Nor did he put you in the time of the Enlightenment or the age of the Classical Greeks.

When I made it to Paris during a layover from Africa in 2012, I had a flash of clarity as I sat in the monstrous shadow of the Eiffel Tower. I wrote this brief passage in my journal:

> I sat there before the tower and looked up at the vast reaches of steel before me. I always imagined I would feel more complete by

the time I made it to Paris, but life did not freeze in some climactic epiphany. Rather, I reminded myself that I am here. Now. And there is presently nowhere else I am, so I should enjoy it, because I will spend a lot of time in my life not being here.

We have a lot to learn from John and Charles Wesley, who founded the Methodist movement in the eighteenth century—a movement which possibly shaped western culture and western Christianity more than any others at the time. The Wesleys were the founding members of a small group at Oxford who called themselves the Holy Club. Another member, John Gambold, wrote about John Wesley, "He had neither the presumption, nor the leisure to anticipate things whose season were not now, and would show some uneasiness whenever any of us…were shifting off the appointed improvement of the present minute." Wesley recognized the importance of being aware of the present so as to be effective as possible, rather than postponing some action or movement.

When I long so badly for the years of my own past, I need to remember that it's not exactly as I remember it. The purity of those first blooming relationships were surely overshadowed by the stress of Pre-Algebra homework and the insecurities that accompany puberty. I'm sure the Ethan living in 2007 was longing for some time other than the one he was in then, just as the Ethan writing this now does.

We also perceive the past through the clarity of the present. I think I'm marginally smarter than I was in eighth grade, so I can look back and see things now that were hidden back then. But longing to go back and live in those years is a fruitless endeavor and a waste of our affections.

Are you missing out on life in the present by wishing it could be 'like it was back in the day'?

I'm going to take it one step further.

There are times when I look back on my walk with God and think to myself, *Man, I wish I could feel as close to God as I did back then!*

I grew up calling myself a Christian. More accurately, I should have called myself a 'Christian stereotype,' as I looked and acted just like a Christian without the substance of a relationship with Jesus. I never did drugs, drank, partied, or even cussed. Jesus probably would have referred to me as a whitewashed tomb: Clean on the outside but pretty rotten on the inside.

At some point in my first year of college, I decided I wanted to do a school with an organization called Youth With A Mission, or YWAM. Did I want to do this because I wanted to help the world, share the gospel, and advance the kingdom of God?

Of course not.

I wanted to travel the world on other people's dime. So I wrote up my support letter and mailed it out to family and friends, earning enough cash to ship myself to Australia for the first stage of the school.

Within a week, I realized this was not what I had signed up for. I expected a bunch of rowdy hippie-ish world travelers who were stoked on experiencing the world and returning home with new crazy stories about their escapades.

What I found were people around my own age who *really* loved Jesus. This was new to me. Almost all the Christians I had known in the past had basically shown up to youth group because it's where their friends were and the games were fun. Sure, we had to sit through the 20-minute message, but it was worth it for the night of antics and cute girls.

But these YWAM people were crazy.

They prayed as if someone were actually listening—Someone who could do something about their requests. They worshipped as if God had really done something spectacular for them, and they told stories of miracles they had seen with their own eyes! I thought things like that were locked away in the annals of biblical history, if they ever happened at all.

Hanging around these YWAM nuts for a few months, God was suddenly no longer a theory or a history lesson to me; He was this real, living, breathing, moving Person who interacted with people and with the world.

We went to Thailand where I saw my first miracle: A demon possessed and crippled man was suddenly healed before my eyes. His wild shrieks stopped and he lay still on the floor of his bamboo hut. From that time on, there was really no turning back for me. God had irreparably ambushed my life. Or rather, He had scooped me up into His life.

My time in that first school was a very humbling and transformative one. I was awakened to the reality of the Lord, and something was stirred up within me that wanted to share this experience of God. So I came home to the States and became a youth pastor at my church. I taught with a fiery passion, eagerly desiring to stir the passion of my high schoolers to the same level of excitement I had for the Word of God and the movement of the Holy Spirit. I began a homeless ministry to share the gospel with people on the streets and tell them they were loved. I feel like I went crazy that whole year because of my fire for the Lord.

And on first observation of that season, I would certainly have appeared to be very close to God. No one would have questioned it.

But I also remember the drives home from a night of youth group, feeling alone, talking to God in the car because He seemed so absent. I called out from the confines of my vehicle, wondering why others seemed to *feel* Him in a way I could not.

I remember wondering why so many other people seemed to have their prayers answered in crazy ways, while I continued to work minimum wage jobs, have no plan for the future and strive for God's affection.

I asked him why the girl I was trying to pursue kept turning me down, despite my most earnest efforts.

I remember beating myself up for not loving God enough, and punished myself by taking away my music and forcing myself to drive in silence, or —possibly the most twisted form of punishment—forcing myself to awkwardly pray for more strangers in public the more I screwed up.

It's easy to idolize our pasts and think times were so much better back then. It's easy to think I was closer to God back then.

Looking back on that season 5 years ago, I can see so many areas I was in err. The zeal I was trying to stir up within the youth group was just that— emotion. Passion. No amount of "authentic worship" (read: putting your hands up, closing your eyes, singing loudly and swaying) will make God love you more. In fact, I would argue that what He really wants from us is honesty. He wants us to cry out alongside the Psalmists, asking where He has gone and why he has removed us from His presence.

I can see that much of the ministry I did with the homeless was done out of pride and ignorance. I knew very little about effective inner city ministry, or how handing out PB&J's enables a problem more than it solves one. I may have been full of fiery passion, but I lacked the wisdom and insight necessary to effectively make a difference.

In the years since then, I have found that an absence of a "feeling" of God doesn't mean God is actually absent. I have learned truth about grace, and how beating myself up and exerting more effort to win God's approval won't really earn me very much. In fact, it will get me nowhere because grace is a gift, and you don't earn gifts.

In the past several years, I've learned how to rest. How to dwell in silence because God lives there just as much as in the wild stories. Silence is a means to a relationship more than a means of punishment.

I say all that to say this: God does not live in the past. He has taken me from that place 5 years ago of being fueled by fiery passion to a more mature place now of peace and contentment, where I can receive His Spirit with open palms instead of working for it with clenched fists. By no means am I a perfected and omniscient Christian, but I've grown and ince 2010.

past, you may see times during which you were closer to God
e now. The fact is, this simply is not true. God brings us
asons to grow us and produce in us good fruit, and if you
thought about it, you would probably see areas in which you are more
mature and nearer to Him now than you were back then. Perpetually
attempting to dwell in the past is a lonely existence. It is a means of
escape from the present, from the people who are near you now, and
from what God is doing in you now.

Longing for the past (or the future) is an escape from intimacy.

The Lord may be trying to teach you something today but you're too
focused on what He did in the past. How can we cultivate intimate
relationships today if we are trying to dwell in the past? I think developing
a sort of 'intimacy with the present' is something we must learn to do.

How many sunsets have you missed because you were too busy
Instagramming them?

Maybe escaping this type of loneliness involves reorienting your nostalgia.
Stir up an intense desire for the bright world looming right next to you
now.

Dwell in a nostalgia for the present, for the time you have been placed in
right now. This is the same conclusion Solomon came to in Ecclesiastes,
to live in the moment and enjoy this life while you have it. You and I will
never know what Paris was like in the 1920's, but we can know what
Colorado is like in 2017; or what Brasil is like in the years after that, or
Hong Kong in the years after that.

Keep your eyes open, because you'll soon be looking back on today and
longing for it.

WANDERLUST

So I'm gonna hop on that train,
I got nowhere to go but no reason to stay.
Maybe I go cause I'm chasing something,
maybe I go cause something is chasing me,
maybe I leave cause I have yet to find someone
to look me in the face and say
Stick around, I want you next to me
so stick around.
-Stick Around by David Ramirez

A couple years ago, I was in a hot tub in Chicago with a beautiful Nigerian girl. She had been reading my blog for a little while before we ever met, so she knew a little bit about my story, though I knew none of hers. She knew my affinity for bouncing about the world.

"What's your favorite road trip you've ever been on?" she asked me as the warm bubbles massaged our backs.

I thought for a moment before answering.

"I'm still on it," I replied with a smirk.

She laughed.

To be honest, that was one of those moments where my inner selves jump-high-fived for thinking of just the right thing to say at just the right time. I thought about how my response made me look poetic and adventurous, which is exactly what I was going for.

And there was a lot of truth in those words: In many ways, though I was still in college at the time, I was unsettled, I had the mentality that I was still drifting through town, I just had to hit pause in Chicago for three years to grab a degree. Then I'd be on my way, the ever-restless wanderer. Life still feels that way most of the time. Since graduating, I've continued to move around, but it feels different now. I'll get to that later though.

A few months ago I was on the beach and feeling restless once more, so I flipped open my Bible app and did a word search of the word "wander." What I found was less than exciting. Here's a sampling of the tone I found for how the Bible uses that word:

> Numbers 32:13—And the LORD's anger was kindled against Israel, and he made them **wander** in the wilderness for forty years...

> 2 Kings 21:8—And I will not cause the feet of Israel to **wander** anymore out of the land that I gave to their fathers...

> Job 12:24—He takes away understanding from the chiefs of the people of the earth and makes them **wander** in a trackless waste.

> Psalm 59:15—They **wander** about for food and growl if they do not get their fill.

> Jeremiah 14:10—They have loved to **wander** thus; they have not restrained their feet; therefore the LORD does not accept them.

Amos 8:12—They shall **wander** from sea to sea, and from north to east; they shall run to and fro, to seek the word of the LORD, but they shall not find it.

It was a sobering moment to realize that this lifestyle I had spent so many years pursuing was used as a punishment 100% of the time in the Bible.

There was not one positive use of that word.

God seemed to punish people who disobeyed or neglected Him by causing them to wander without a purpose. He unsettled them and made them transient and rootless.

On the other hand, The Lord *rewarded* people by giving them land to settle on. He gives the Israelites the Promised Land to inhabit (after cursing them by making them *wander* in the wilderness for forty years; a trip that should have taken two weeks). Abraham, Isaac and Noah are all given land to settle. God blessed King David and lets his son Solomon build a home in their kingdom.

Ironically it is Jesus, the Man of Sorrows, who has no place to lay his head and wanders like a vagrant during the three years of his ministry.

Our culture has shifted in recent decades, encouraging a life of noncommittal freedom and travel as a means of fulfillment. Books like Elizabeth Gilbert's *Eat, Pray, Love* encourage an abandonment of responsibility and an indefinite jaunt around the globe in order to find some new kind of satisfaction. My music library is bursting with songs about walking out, hitting the road, and tasting freedom.

Look at this verse by Matt Costa taken from his song The Road. He stirs up feelings of angst and wanting to leave, imagining how much better life on the road will be:

> Don't talk, don't say nothing
> I just packed my bags

and I'm heading for something
Where I'm going, well I don't really know,
the road is calling and I've got to go.

A few verses later though, Costa reveals a more somber look at the cost of living this way.

Don't talk, don't say nothing.
I just grabbed my things
and pretend like there's nothing
between us no more
as I walked out the door.
She closed it behind me and cried on the floor
and I couldn't talk,
no I couldn't say nothing
I just closed my eyes
and head blindly toward something.

The tone of the song is so light and optimistic that for years I missed what he was really saying in this song. When we leave and hit the road searching for liberty and new opportunities, there are people we leave behind. People who cry on the floor once we take off. The restless, rootless life is not as glamorous as it is typically portrayed.

When I first arrived at Moody Bible Institute, the routine and structure of the school ground hard against my soul. I had just come from a wild summer of being homeless on the beach, teaching stand-up paddleboard lessons and sleeping under the stars. I had made it a point to be in the ocean every single day of that summer, even on days I wasn't working. My skin was tanned darker than midnight and I had sand permanently lodged in every cranny of my body.

It was amazing.

I even had to make a few trips to Nigeria over the course of the summer as well. And prior to that, I was bouncing around between Boston and New Hampshire, sleeping in church basements and enjoying the mystery of every unfolding day.

So in the fall when I strolled onto Moody's Chicago campus in my short cut-off jean shorts and tank top, I could not have felt more like an alien. Not only was I an outsider to the conservative culture of one of the top Bible schools in the world, but the daily routine and responsibility had become foreign to me. Waking up and making it to class, following the dress code and bending the knee to a handful of arbitrary rules felt like throwing sand into the gears of my humanity. I couldn't function. Any day, I thought, I'd seriously snap and go off the rails.

And apparently I talked about leaving a lot within the first couple weeks I was there. Not only did I endlessly talk about my past escapades and adventures, but I continually brought up the fact that I probably couldn't last in Chicago and I would ship out any day.

Which is why one day I sat in Starbucks with one of the guys on my floor and listened to him tell me why he couldn't get close to me as a friend.

"I just feel like I can't invest in you too much as a friend because you keep talking about leaving," he gently explained. "I want to. I want to get to know you and become good friends but I can't because in the back of my mind, I just feel like you're gonna take off."

I don't remember my response to him, but looking back, I think that conversation altered the way I pursued relationships. It made me realize that if I'm willing to put effort into relationships, people are equally willing to give back to me. And they want to. We all want relationships where we can both give and receive on deep levels. But if our mindset is one of being ready to hit the road and float away, it is impossible to create any kind of meaningful relationships.

In his incredibly existential book *The Unbearable Lightness of Being*, Milan Kundera posits that the more connected we are to those around us, the more weighed down we are. Therefore, every person is presented with two options: Commit yourself to no one and be free as an untethered balloon, or love those around you and become 'weighed down' by the responsibility of loving other people. Kundera likely had no idea how the former would come to dominate our culture in the ensuing years, and how noncommittal relationships and rampant divorces would become the new norm.

A free floating person may well be free, but they are incredibly lonely.

Kundera even observes at one point in the book, "A person who longs to leave the place where he lives is an unhappy person."

Perhaps you are more inclined to the comfort of home and the peace that comes with familiarity and routine. You may not have a burning desire to travel the world or get up and move. In today's culture however, it is just as possible to have the mentality of a wanderer without ever leaving your apartment.

One of my all-time favorite films is *Beginners,* and in one scene, the lachrymose protagonist is lying in bed next to his new French girlfriend. As an actress, she embodies the spirit of the traveler with no roots, just a few belongings she slings from one luxurious hotel room to the next.

"I used to love hotels," she tells him across the pillow. "Now I'm always in a new apartment or in another hotel somewhere."

"How do you keep hold of friends?" he asks. "Or boyfriends?"

"Makes it very easy to end up alone. To leave people," she replies.

He thinks for a moment and then says, "You can stay in the same place and still find ways to leave people."

The reality is, many of us live this way even if we have lived in the same town our entire lives. You don't have to travel the world to be far away from someone else, nor do you have to move to a new city to cut off a relationship. I think the anemic nature of many of our relationships reflects a fear of commitment, a longing to depart and not be tied down, whether geographically or just emotionally.

Mark Sayers, in his masterful book *The Road Trip That Changed The World*, documents this spirit of wander and lays the lion share of the blame at the feet of Jack Kerouac, Neal Cassidy and their crew of vagabond Beat poets. He points out just how this notion of *the road* has come to define modern culture. Everything is seen as a journey of some sort, and being rootless and vagrant is praised.

Sayers spends an entire chapter describing how the car and the road changed nearly every aspect of modern life. For instance, there was hardly a concept of premarital sex prior to the automobile, as finding a spouse was a familial and communal event, done in the context of both people's families, or tribes, and getting alone for an opportunity to hook up was a foreign concept.

In a similar fashion, fast food emerged as a result of the automobile. Prior to the Model T, food was always prepared with care in the home, or in exquisite sit-down restaurants. After the emergence of the automobile however, foodies wanted to cook up ways to eat chicken while on the road. Thus, the chicken nugget was born. There was even an unspoken race to find the right recipe that would make eating on-the-go the most convenient.

This concept of the road as a way of life is so engrained into our culture that we don't even realize it today. Kerouac and his pals paved the way for an entirely new subculture to emerge—the cool, mysterious vagabond. The world traveler. The free-spirited wanderer. These characters seem commonplace to us today, but in the middle of last century, the Beat poets were rewriting the way life could be lived, and we are currently living in the fallout.

Steven Bouma-Prediger and Brian J. Walsh compare the trials of third-world refugees to this sect of middle-class Western wanderers. In some ways, the Westerners have sought out what characterizes refugees, such as rootlessness, having all their things in one backpack, and the like. Bouma-Prediger describes these Westerners as traveling the world, fleeing relationships, changing jobs, and always on the move—yet suffering a poverty of meaning, a loss of true home, identity, and place. They describe it as a psychic homelessness which lacks a true spiritual home.

The issue is not that these individuals (such as myself) travel—and enjoy traveling—the world and seeing new sights and engaging in new experiences. The trouble comes when we realize we are unable to set down deep roots, both in people and in places. It's an issue when travel is turned to as a purpose-giving fountain, where identity and meaning are freely distributed like candy at a parade.

As the chorus of *Moab*, one of my favorite Mystic Valley Band songs asserts, "There is nothing that the road cannot heal." This mindset of escape and travel has become widespread yet under-realized by modern society. In fact, it is often praised and romanticized by people unaware of the emotionally evasive roots of this transient problem, and unable to think logically through the results of such a lifestyle.

I'm not talking about family vacations or basking in the otherness of a new culture. I still travel a lot for various photography and speaking engagements, and I love it. I sometimes feel guilty for loving trips to so many parts of the world and meeting so many different people. What I'm talking about is an inescapable attraction to wandering.

Rootlessness.

Transience.

The idea that I will be more fulfilled and my purpose will be realized only on the open road.

I was talking about this today with my friend Megan, who is a kindred soul in regards to perpetual voyaging. In fact, let me share a story about just how itinerant she and I were at one point.

In the spring of 2012, I had decided to head to Boston to answer a call for help at the YWAM base there. They had just bought a new building—a gigantic old funeral home in Somerville—and needed help renovating it. I threw everything I owned into a big backpack and went east. It was an awkward start to a season, as I had loosely talked to one of the staff members on the phone and mentioned that I would *probably* be coming soon, and then a few weeks later, I showed up at their front door, ready to move in.

Once everything was sorted out, I was led upstairs by one of the base staff. She showed me my bunk and a dresser where I could unpack all my clothes and make myself at home. She then left me alone to move in. I unloaded all my belongings, getting as settled as possible in the spacious room with four other bunks. Once I felt unpacked enough, I went downstairs and began to introduce myself to the rest of the students and staff at the base.

About two hours after I had moved in and unpacked all my earthly belongings, the director of the base called an all-staff meeting. We congregated into a big circle and he began to explain that the fire marshal had just been walking around the building, and deemed the building unlivable while the renovations were taking place.

We had 24 hours to evacuate the building.

Less than two hours after arriving at this new home, I was being kicked out. The base director went on to tell us that they were still working on the details, but we would be living in church basements during the week, and on the weekend, we'd be trekking up north to New Hampshire to stay with various host families who were willing to open their homes to us. Essentially, for several months, our homes would become our backpacks and the vans toting us to and fro.

ple, upon hearing this news would bemoan the loss of stability sical notion of 'home', but YWAMers are a unique breed. Not only were we accepting of the changes, but we cheered when the director told us we would suddenly be homeless.

I can't speak for everyone in that circle, but I think I had this romanticized ideal of freedom and a millennial wanderlust resting in my bones. I wanted to flee the outdated concepts of settling down and committing to a sedentary life in exchange for a life of high-adrenaline story chasing.

Megan was in that circle and I remember seeing her smile at the idea of bouncing around and laying her head in a different place every night. Today I was talking with her about this idea of wanderlust being a poisonous pursuit of something that isn't real. In a characteristically long text message she shared some similar thoughts she had been having.

> One of the big (and should have been obvious) things I realized in school was that all the trips I went on, friends I visited, and even missions trips I was a part of gave me a false sense of what life could look like. I was traveling from farm to farm eating the perfect fruit in season everywhere I went, but I never noticed the planting and watering and weeding day after day after day that made the fruit grow. I would have thought farming was just eating fruit all day and I would have been so wrong. I went home and was so annoyed with paper writing and email sending and not being able to grocery shop until I ate the food already in my fridge.

> I want to jump to the end of things; or at least I want things to take less time than they do: Jump straight from meeting someone to becoming easy, deep, well-known friends. Skip awkwardly dating people and magically wake up married. Fast forward July-September so I can always be working on missions trips at work but that's not how life works. And it's not about what I want or how I feel every day, and there's a meaning and purpose and truth

that's flowing constantly under all those things, and I don't want to miss it fleeing from "one passion to the next." When you accept the truth of things and seasons and time, you slowly realize there's a lot of goodness in the in-between and day-to-day life. And the best things you have and value are the ones you've earned, built, cultivated, and been without.

I love the imagery she used of wanting the fruit but not the work required to grow the fruit. Food does not just pop into existence, especially good food. It takes a lot of time and effort to cultivate good, tasty peaches or sweetcorn or lentils. In many ways, our modern food industry echoes the idea of instant gratification and cheaper products in order to contribute to the speedy pace of our on-the-go lives.

I remember being a boy and growing our own Halloween pumpkins in the back yard, as well as onions, cucumbers, and sunflowers. I remember coming home from school and checking on them every day, seeing how much they've grown and which fruits were getting close to ripe. How symbolic is that? We don't want to have patience for good food to grow because we prefer the cheaper, easier substitute. Many of us don't want to wait for rich relationships to develop so we whittle away our time on the cheap substitute of social media or nightlife.

Today, that idea of care and patient cultivation has become foreign to me. I want to be on the interstate at midnight, stopping to grab a gas station hot dog that's been on those hot silver rollers for a few hours.

Because it's fast and easy and tastes good.

Because the image of being on the road in the middle of the night is so *rock'n roll*.

Because wherever I'm going isn't as enjoyable as the journey to get there.

"The experience of the journey trumps the importance of the destination," writes Mark Sayers.

As idealized as it is in today's media, the life of the wandering explorer is a lonely one. From personal experience, I can tell you that movies don't convey the painful longing wrapped into every phone call home to both family and friends. They don't show how lonely the hotel or hostel rooms are, even when filled with likeminded travelers who are still essentially strangers, "Single-serving friends," as *Fight Club* calls them.

There was this one time I was in a crowded hostel in Australia. The co-ed rooms each had three bunk beds, enough for six people. I noticed that one of the beds was being shared by a chubby English couple, meaning there were seven people sleeping on six tiny mattresses in one room.

There were several nights I was awakened by odd things while staying in that hostel, including the English couple...'bumping crumpets' in the room full of strangers. Another night I was stirred from sleep by another woman's boyfriend climbing in through the window.

Hostel rooms have taught me that even sleeping in the same room as half a dozen others is no escape from loneliness.

A few years ago when I was still in the desperate throes of wanderlust, I had a conversation with one of my cousins. He has a similar background to mine—he has spent months at a time traveling and doing missions work in various countries—but he is now married, has two children, and pastors a church in a small town in Ohio. I was complaining to him about the angst in my bones that didn't want, but *needed* to leave the country and see more.

"I know you won't believe me right now," he told me, "but having a family is better than traveling. It is so much more fulfilling and satisfying."

Of course I won't know if he was right for a while, but it makes logical sense. Marriage and parenthood take work—lots of work—but the benefits are just like the giant pumpkins that emerged from the ground in my back yard. With time and care come giant rewards. But when I travel in order to find purpose or happiness, there are no seeds sown, and therefore no meaningful rewards reaped. There are no roots that develop between me and other places or people. Deep relationships take time, and this cannot happen when our hearts are set on departure and scanning the globe in search of meaning and happiness.

It seems that real happiness takes work but we're content to settle for shortcuts.

In many ways, traveling is a shortcut to happiness. The momentary thrill it provides is overshadowed by the knowledge that everything we create is temporary and every adventure will end with a melancholy flight home to the loneliness we were avoiding in the first place.

We've come up with this notion of 'finding yourself' while wandering about. Not only is this a relatively new concept, but I would contend that it is outright unbiblical. The Bible presents everything as best when it is rooted in a healthy community. We will be most productive and satisfied when we are surrounded by a community of others; when they are giving to us and we get to give back to the community. The notion of wandering about in order to 'find ourselves' is not only hyper-individualistic, but it is unsustainable and abstract. As Christians, we should be rooted in our local church.

When I grew sunflowers as a boy, they didn't get up and wander around my backyard, though we've all probably had nightmares like that. No plant can grow when it is uprooted and connected to nothing but the air. In the same way, people are made for community. If we think of our local church as the soil where we receive nutrients and are given a safe place to grow, it makes sense that we should want to stay. Just like the sunflowers, growing a healthy community takes time. Gardens don't pop up overnight, but take careful work and patience.

Part of the problem is that churches have hurt us. They are made up of imperfect people who may have alienated us or condemned us.

The question is, are we going to respond in kind and move away from those people, or will we move *toward* them, even after pain and offense? Will we make an effort to build strong relationships, even where people may have hurt us, or will we retreat, assuming other people somewhere else will be better? (Of course sometimes that's the case and there are people we should leave in the past. But I'm speaking to the majority of us who are wounded and then retreat while there is still opportunity for healing and growth.)

Perhaps you're like my friend who I'll call Darwin. Darwin is one of my dearest friends, and part of the reason we *get* each other is because we both have the soul of untethered kites, flying hither and yon. As I write this, he is hitchhiking somewhere between Montana and California.

Darwin was actually with me on the beach the day I searched the Bible for the word 'wander.' I brought it up to him for his thoughts, and over the course of the ensuing conversation, Darwin explained to me why he feels the need to constantly uproot and leave.

"I've been to a lot of churches," he said. "And every time I go to a new church, I love to take the body and blood of Christ. I love the Word. I love communally worshipping God with fellow believers. Church is good."

Darwin's face was sad as he continued.

"But when I'm at a church, I see so many great and loving people working together to make church happen. And then I realize that there is nothing I have that I can contribute to a church."

I protested that he has plenty to offer a church, and began listing off his great attributes.

"You say those things," he cut me off, "But internally, I constantly feel like I have nothing to offer anyone. There is nothing I can give to a community from which they would benefit. So I just leave. They don't need me."

As much as I disagreed with Darwin's notion that he had nothing to offer, I had to admit that I often had the same feelings. There have been countless times I've seen gifted people in churches and organizations doing amazing things, at which point I begin to think about how little I have to offer.

These feelings of inadequacy have often contributed to my flights around the globe. *If I can't be of service here, I should go hold orphans in Haiti. THEN I'll be useful.*

The truth is, it's a lie that we are not good enough to contribute to a community. I would imagine most of us feel inadequate—like we have nothing to offer—at times, and these feelings affect our actions. We withhold ourselves from others because we feel insufficient as human beings. I'm going to get into this more in a later chapter, but for now, just know that the devil tries to deceive us by telling us we are useless. He wants us to uproot and leave constantly rather than giving to a healthy community and receiving from that same group of people. We are all broken and have our own struggles, but giving in to thoughts that you are useless benefits no one, most of all, yourself.

I'm not poo-pooing travel because I'm a grump.

Believe me, no one wants to pack up and leave more than I do. But after years of incarnating this mindset, I have realized how unhealthy it is, and how it has stunted my spiritual growth. Because of my constant motion, I have not been able to disciple younger people as I should have, nor have I had older men pour into me. I may have seen the world, but I have missed out on opportunities to mature.

I keep moving now, but not because I love the road like I used to. I still travel a lot, but now there is more direction behind it. My actions aren't filled with desperation as much as they are with mission and purpose. I'm not fleeing anything anymore, I'm slowly putting down roots, and finding people who will volunteer to be the soil. Because God knows there's no home without people, and every relationship of any kind is an experiment. We have to take a risk.

So I'm still on the greatest road trip of my life.

We all are in many ways.

I think the trick is to learn how to put roots down where you can, in whom you can. I used to be so scared of being known, of settling down and letting myself be planted in one place. Travel is not the problem, fear is. Fear of being known and loved, or perhaps fear of commitment.

I used to love being the new, mysterious guy who has traveled the world and was simply passing through town like a breeze in an alley. There is a cool aura emitted from this kind of persona; it's an adventurous life for sure. But I have found that people can't be intimate with a mystery.

If we want to move toward intimacy, we have to give up mystery.

Don't look to travel as a cure to pain and struggles in your life, or a way to escape from them. At best, it will only prolong your loneliness and lack of intimacy. At worst, it will turn you in on yourself, making you even more distant and unknowable to those you encounter. I've been there, and believe me, it's not as glamorous as it looks.

Within the first couple of weeks at college, when I was deeply feeling the urge to move on once more, I penned this song in the back of my notebook during a ministry class. As catchy as it is to sing along to, it embodies the soul of longing to uproot and leave, to float like a cloud atop the surface of the earth.

The Nomad's Anthem

Oh I've got that bug, I got that wandering bug again
It's itching at my foot soles and its gnawing on my head
I've got to fly, I've got to dip, I've think I've got somewhere to be
But girl you know your pretty lips already did so much for me
But there's a soul inside my skin he thinks he's Christopher Columbus,
Gotta sail he's gotta run before he's just college alumnus
Girl you know I can't sit still, I'm restless like the waves.
They roll and move and tend to lose more ground now every day

(Chorus)
I know I'll find it, I'll find it someday
By plane, car, greyhound, or the New York subway
And when I get there, I'll take my boots off,
I'll last a few days, Then probably move on

I got a call the other day, the road's lonely once more.
He said that he remembers me like ships remember shores.
I sat down here and planted roots, it was an accident I swear.
Because no matter where I am, I long for over there.

(Chorus)

This city's walls have dried me out like a starfish on the rock
And though the lake is near, the coast is much too far to walk.
The ocean is my home, it is my permanent address.
Cause if home is where the heart is, there's salt water in my chest.

(Chorus)

OPERATION: ACOUSTIC KITTY

"You can't just sit there and put everybody's lives ahead of yours and think that counts as love."
-The Perks of Being a Wallflower

In the mid-1960's, the CIA launched an operation called Acoustic Kitty.

This was the time everyone was spying on everyone, so every room was bugged. Every conference room was unsafe to share secrets. The USA was bugging the hotels of the Soviets, and the kremlin was doing the same to us. As a result, the only safe place to have a private conversation became outside in public places, surrounded by strangers and drowned out by the sounds of the crowds. Agents would meet in parks or on sidewalks where the noise of the traffic and pedestrians would disguise their top-secret discussions.

The CIA was desperate to figure out a way to get intel on these public, yet inaccessible conversations. They couldn't bug every single square foot of the world, so they had to get creative. And what they came up with was Operation Acoustic Kitty.

Again, this is a true story.

The idea was, no one would notice a cat strolling through a park or pay much attention when it came close to a group of men having a talk. The Soviets would never think to beware of cats while meeting in public squares for a rendezvous.

The main reason cats were such a good idea, thought the CIA, is because they can't be trained. No one would suspect them as they would suspect a pigeon or a dog, because no one could ever train cats. They go where they want and do as they please.

Of course, this was also the primary problem the CIA had in training their battalion of feline spies. The cats couldn't be trained to to go where the operatives wanted them to, so the employees had to get even more creative.

Over the course of their experimentation, they found that they could control the cat to a small degree using electrical currents that would zap the cat toward their intended destination. It wasn't quite the enormous success they had hoped for, but they somehow rigged a way to get the cat to move in a general direction. I love the way the declassified document puts it: They declared it a "remarkable scientific achievement...knowing that cats can indeed be trained to move short distances."

Yes, it is remarkable to make an animal move a short distance.

This was the age before PETA, so the agents were slicing open the cats, inserting wires and microphones under their fur. The microphone came up through the skin somewhere around the cat's neck, and the tail was used as the transmitting antenna. Crammed full of wires and radio parts, the cat would ideally stroll where the CIA directed it with electrical zaps, picking up Kremlin conversations in public places.

All told, the operation took several years and cost the USA $20 million to develop this Agent Kitty.

Which is why it was such a tremendous disappointment when the day finally came to put the cat to use. He was released from the CIA van and got hit by a taxi while crossing the street. $20 million down the drain along with years of scientific research and slicing and sewing of cats.

Don't we all have Agent Kitty days?

If I'm honest, I feel like this is how so many of my relationships turn out. I put in so much effort to try to build a friendship, but the efforts are often in vain.

Something I learned about myself recently is that I'm a pretty intense person. There have been times I've walked up to someone and said, "Hey, we're going to be friends now, okay?" I'd say it works about half the time. Some of my best friendships have come from intentional moves like that, while other people have been scared off by such direct confrontation.

I'm also the type of person who wants to hang out all the time.

Every day.

Every hour.

I'm a quality *and* quantity time person, on top of being a big time extrovert. Being around people is my jam. So when I invest a lot of time into someone, only to have them blow me off, change plans, or simply drift away from a relationship, it hurts.

I wouldn't quite compare it to being sliced open, filled with wires, sewn back up and hit by a taxi, but still...

I've seen this pattern ever since high school. I had one friend who would always make plans with me for a fun sleepover on Friday night, only to change his mind at the last minute. *"Because he didn't feel like it."* I think the notion that I have to beg and force people to hang out with me is a mindset that emerged from a series of rejections and has held on to this day. So now, when someone cancels a plan to get together, I must consciously remind myself that it's not personal. It's not that no one wants to hang out with me; I'm just an extrovert and not everyone wants to be with friends 24/7.

Perhaps your story looks a little different. I'm sure we can all name times we have put ample amounts of effort into a relationship—platonic or romantic—only to see our efforts crushed in the end. Maybe you worked really hard on a gift for someone and they hated it. Perhaps you're the type of person who shows love to people by serving them, only to have your actions go unnoticed.

The past couple years, I've realized that many of the things I do in order to win friends have really been selfish in nature. Rather than spending time becoming a better friend—someone people will *want* to hang out with all the time, I simply tried to escape being alone by begging people to hang out with me. Essentially, my motives for spending time with people were selfish. I didn't want to serve them as much as I wanted to use them as an escape from being alone.

It never feels good when people use us simply as a means to an end.

I spent so much time pursuing friends that I never stopped to ask myself if I'm the type of person people want to hang out with. We all like to be around people who are selfless and genuinely care about us, but I feel like we put too little effort into becoming those people.

In his timeless book *How to Win Friends and Influence People*, Dale Carnegie writes that "You can make more friends in two months by being interested in other people than in two years of trying to get people interested in you." Hopefully you're the type of person who reads that and says *Duh!* For some reason, it took me nearly a quarter century to realize this basic truth.

In other words, trying to get people to like you by showing off or selfishly forcing them to hang with you is like trying to train a cat to be a spy.

Part of the reason I've felt lonely so often is because I wasn't the type of person many people wanted to be with. Sure, I always wanted to hang out, but my motives were more Ethan-centric than they were others-centered. I wanted to talk about my own life and thoughts more than I wanted to hear about my friends.

If you're one of those people who persistently catches yourself talking about yourself when you're around other people, try to become more aware of the topics of your conversations. How well do you know what's going on in your friends' lives? What's the weather like inside your boyfriend's heart? How are Ruth's parents?

Learning to undo selfishness is possibly the hardest fight in life, since our nature is programmed to focus exclusively on ourselves. In building relationships, try to find ways to put others first. Focus on them and their lives more than your own. Wait for them to ask about you before spouting off about yourself. It's something I'm still learning to do, but it's already more rewarding than being fixated on myself.

I think one aspect of community I've long overlooked is the reality of Christian community versus my expectations. What I mean is, I have some ethereal and perfect image in my head of what my friend group should look like, and it never seems to line up with my real friends. I envision attractive people dressed like hipsters moving in slow motion at some party, eating good food and laughing a lot. Strings of mini Edison Bulbs line the corners of our rooms. We never fight and always encourage each other.

But when I look at my list of friends, they are real people. They are flawed, imperfect and quirky. We fight sometimes, and a lot of times I drive home alone feeling unsatisfied, wondering why my collection of friends doesn't look like the imaginary gang of magazine models I imagined in my head.

I passed through high school and my experiences never looked like those

of the Disney and Nickelodeon characters. I went tc
my classmates never seemed *quite* as awesome as those
you think of wild college days. It seemed like everyone ε
experience of college and came out with lifelong friends w
and never fight.

Of course I graduated college with great friends, many of whc ↄ still talk to and love. The problem is, unlike the imaginary people in my head, they are flawed, imperfect, and human. They're nothing like the college pals I had previously prophesied.

Now, I've kind of been an adult for a few years and my adulthood doesn't look like everyone else's. Where are the frequent dinner parties illuminated by artsy string lights and the idyllic camping trips in the mountains? Where is my girlfriend? My wife?

Life hasn't ever really gone the way I predicted it would, and rather than appreciate the surprising beauty of this, I let it create a sort of cognitive dissonance inside me. There has been friction between my forecast of life and what really ends up happening. Dietrich Bonhoeffer puts it succinctly in his book *Life Together*:

> "Those who love their dream of a Christian community more than the Christian community itself become destroyers of that Christian community even though their personal intentions may be ever so honest, earnest, and sacrificial."

It's toxic when we love our ideas of community, fellowship and friendship more than we love the actual people around us. It creates a form of internal thunder when the high-pressure systems of our imaginations collide with the low-pressure reality of the very real, smelly people around us and the two don't get along.

It's lonely when the people we imagine are closer to us than the real people in our lives.

For this reason, I've almost come to detest the word *community*. It is so

...act and impersonal. I think Christians especially are guilty of tossing it around like mashed potatoes in the camp mess hall. It's thin and flimsy and doesn't mean much when it's not associated with real people. Churches may spout the benefits of their 'community' and how beneficial their 'community' is, but what good is this abstract idea if it is not tied to reality? To actual human beings?

Recently, my pastor in Denver called out our congregation for exactly this. He said there was a couple in the church who had been pregnant and lost the baby, but not a single person from the church came to visit them, bring them food or even just sit with them in their deep grief.

When we spout off about the wonderful concept of community but do not put in the effort to make it a reality, nothing happens and more people end up lonely and hurting. Like the couple in my church who lost their child, there are times we desperately need others. Yet when others are too busy or consumed in their own lives to reach out and sacrifice, a gaping lack of love is shown.

We don't know love because we don't know sacrifice.

The world is hungry for the love of Christ, and this is shown through Christians who are willing to sacrifice for others. Perhaps our Christian communities and churches would be more appealing if we recognized them as real people with real needs and real wounds, rather than concepts of idealistic communes. This is what Jesus meant in John 13:34 when He said that the world will know us by our love. He wants us to love one another in such a way that the world sees and gets jealous of the love we have for one another.

When was the last time you heard a church described that way by a non-Christian?

It's easy to love our own dreams and visions of the ideal community. It's much harder to love the

broken,

fallen,

sinful,

hurting,

needy,

real

people around you. Yet if we want any hope of escaping loneliness and engaging in real intimacy, we must put our abstract communal ideas aside and put in work to love people around us. It can be as simple as inviting someone to coffee—especially someone who doesn't get asked to coffee very often.

Community is usually not as pretty and blissful as we hope, but I think with work and appreciation of the real people around us, and the relationships that exist in our lives, we can work toward authentic community. The beauty of real relationships versus imagined ones is not an aesthetic one. Your life probably won't look like a happy episode of *Friends*, nor will your friends always look as flawless and attractive.

The beauty of real relationships is that they're real.

I love the short monologue from the character Paul in the film *500 Days of Summer*. He is asked about his dream girl and how his wife compares to her. He replies,

> "I think technically 'The Girl Of My Dreams' would probably have, like, a really bodacious rack, you know? Maybe different hair. She'd probably be a little more into sports. But truthfully, Robyn is better than the girl of my dreams…She's real."

I love how simply he puts it. No matter how we envision the people we *want* around us, choosing to love the *real* people around us will always be better. Just because they're real.

I have a pen pal of sorts, and recently she recounted a similar thought, only in a more poetic and romantic way. I had previously written to her regarding a woman I was interested in and she replied thus:

> How is your person? Karen...no Karry? Or is it with and "ie"? Have you had to reformulate your rhetoric of relating yet? People tend to mess up the ideas we've carefully laid.
>
> Like Will.
>
> I thought he was good because he was good in some ways. I forget that people are not flat, they have dimensions and I try to wrap my own world around them without realizing the cost that might accrue. But hey, I scraped by Algebra 101 with a C and that includes weekly tutoring. So yeah, I've never been one to "count up the cost" very well anyway.

Many of our problems with relationships come from the expectations we project onto others. We have this idea of what our boyfriend or girlfriend will be like, then when they don't fit into that mold, we are disappointed. The same is true of marriage and even our circles of friends.

This dichotomy between our expectations and our reality leads not only to cognitive dissonance, but loneliness as well. When we can't connect to people as they are, in their current condition, we end up more distant from them and unable to relate. If we truly want intimacy with others, we need to set aside our notions of what our friends and family *should* look like and embrace them as they are, here and now.

Are we being realistic and practical in our approach to loving others, or are we trying to train cats to be spies?

FAME, INTIMACY AND HOT MONKEYS

"But you don't wanna be high like me
Never really knowing why like me
You don't ever wanna step off that roller coaster
And be all alone"
-Mike Posner, *I Took a Pill in Ibiza*

One of my college writing professors once told the class that good runners develop a metered sort of rhythm as the soles of their shoes hit the pavement.

pit-pit   pit-pit

I've heard this pattern many times while running and the evening of December 13, 2015 was no exception. I can only hear the rhythm of my strides when I run without music, and this evening the pouring rain had forced me to leave all electronics indoors.

I was in Chicago for a visit to my alma mater, Moody Bible Institute, and set out for an evening run *because* it was raining, not in spite of it. The midwest was having unseasonably warm weather that month, so I didn't even need a shirt.

I traversed east to the lakefront where the raindrops became millions of tiny percussive beads punching into Lake Michigan. The warm drips surrounded and swallowed me as my shoes contacted the pavement in that familiar beat, more wet sounding than usual.

pish-pish pish-pish

I covered mile after familiar mile, as this was the trail I had run all three years of college. I was totally alone thanks to the weather. Chicagoans may be immune to frigid February temperatures, but the wet wet rain tends to drive them indoors.

Which is why it was odd when I ran the inlet from Oak Street Beach up to North Avenue and spotted a news van preparing to go live right there on the lakefront. I curiously ran to the vehicle and found some men preparing for a broadcast, all their backs turned away from me into the van.

"What are you reporting on?" I asked, indicating the emptiness of the beachfront.

Without turning around, the reporter answered, "We're just doing a bit on this unusually warm weather." A moment later he turned and looked at me, shirtless and thoroughly soaked. "Man!" he said, "You would be perfect for this! Look," he shouted to the cameraman, "this guy doesn't even have a shirt on!" Then, back to me, "If you want to wait 20 minutes, you can be on TV for a couple seconds. I could interview you."

I thought about this, and how fun it would be to send my parents and friends the video of me on the news. But then I realized the evening was getting cooler and standing there for 20 minutes would result in uncontrollable shivers and wasted time.

I thanked him for the offer and began running back to campus.

Five minutes down the path, something was nagging at me. I hate turning down any kind of fun and unique opportunity, so I stopped the *pish-pish* of my waterlogged sneakers and turned back to the van. When I arrived, I asked if the offer to be on TV still stood.

"Sure," the reporter told me. "Come stand right here, we're going live in two minutes." I stood beside the well dressed and warm reporter, shirtless, slightly shivering, and mildly out of breath.

As I chatted with the him while we waited for the finger cue from the cameraman he asked what I wanted to say. I told him I wanted to say I was single, and he burst into laughter. "That's a good one," he admitted, not believing for a second I was serious.

Finally, the cameraman pointed up, then right at us and we were live.

The video was captured.

Not a minute later, I was jogging away from the van, chuckling to myself and hoping I would be able to find the video online to show my family. The run back took fifteen minutes. I dripped into the dorm building and up the stairs to my friend's room.

"I was just on TV!" I told him when I came through the door. I opened a laptop and found WGN's site. Small waves of excitement pulsed through me when I saw myself large and centered on their home page. I took a picture of it so I would always remember the day I was on this local television station's home page.

Then I went on Facebook.

In the 20 minutes since its creation, the video had earned 24,000 views. People were sharing it like mono and I got more excited, still not knowing just how big this video would be or how it would alter the direction of my life.

Some of the guys from the dorm went to get sushi and as we ate, we watched on our phones as the view count rose by the tens of thousands. When I got back, my phone was going crazy with notifications and then the news station called. They wanted me back for the 9pm news and again for the morning show. The guys I was with were screaming. I was screaming. This was completely foreign to all of us.

That Sunday night was the beginning of the most surreal week of my life. MTV dubbed my run *the jog seen 'round the world*. CBS referred to me as 'the sexiest man on earth.' Ethan the Shirtless Runner appeared on national television, national Australian television, and national Canadian television. I was interviewed on TV 12 times that week. A limo picked me up for one of those broadcasts. GQ and Cosmopolitan interviewed me for dating advice. The reporter from TIME flirted with me and said to come visit her in New York, and multiple sassy radio personalities made off-color jokes while we were live on the air together.

On top of the media attention, women (and men) friend requested me by the thousands and sent messages, praising my blog, my personality, my appearance, and even proposing to marry me. People around the world speculated about my sexual orientation, grooming habits, religious views and more.

Then the invites to move to Los Angeles and be on television came, including a message from one of the Kardashian's publicists.

So I went.

I shot across the country in my beat up Corolla into the heart of the entertainment industry. I bumped elbows (literally one time) with movie stars, had Bible studies with YouTube celebrities and met Fabio at a sushi bar.

My friends—and even the president of Moody—referred to me as 'Mr. Celebrity,' and from the outside, it appeared that my life had finally crested that golden plateau of acclaim and satisfaction. I had finally *made it*.

My interior life was a different story, however.

While the masses fawned over my 28-second interview, I subconsciously found myself depending on the digital feedback of others. Numbers of Likes and approving compliments were my lifeblood, but one negative comment would wreck me. When I had a new interview or television appearance, I was elated, but then it would end, the cameras would click off and the technician would come collect my earpiece and mic.

People knew my name but didn't know *me*.

They may know what I look like shirtless, but they don't know what makes me tick. We don't have inside jokes or a history of crazy stories together. They don't know what makes me lose my temper, or what breaks my heart. They've never held me as I cried, and they certainly don't know if I'm quality marriage material.

We humans have this innate desire to be known and loved, and the age of social media has preyed upon this fact. It has offered a shortcut to intimacy in some respects, allowing certain online posts to collect hundreds of Likes, while others garner only a pitiful handful. Those posts that receive better feedback subliminally tell us we are finally worthy, we have worth...today.

But wait and see what you post tomorrow...

Wait and see how *it* will do.

Receiving a sudden deluge of attention showed me that our desires for intimacy have become displaced. Rather than seek out deeper relationships with our close friends and family, we crave higher follower counts and greater digital approval. Ecclesiastes 1:8 has been proved true once more: The eye never has its fill of seeing, nor the ear its fill of hearing, nor the Twitter its fill of retweets.

This is important to note today more than ever before, since roughly 40% of younger generations have stated that they would like to be famous some day, and their lives will be more meaningful if they can achieve a certain level of notoriety. In a survey I gave at one high school, a tenth grader wrote that "Fame is everything to me. Being famous is my number 2 goal." (Sadly, he did not include what his number one goal is, so let's assume it's getting a really good perm.)

Donald Fairbairn wrote in his book *Life in the Trinity* that the most "insidious effect" of America's celebrity culture is its "constant, subliminal message that we are not really important." That you are no one unless you make it. If celebrities are the gods of this age, what does that make the rest of us "normal" people? We take selfies with the famous in order to attach ourselves to someone or something of worth, rather than see ourselves as having intrinsic value.

Facebook subliminally tells us that we are only worthwhile if our statuses and photos receive rave reviews. Even Mark Zuckerberg, Facebook's founder and CEO, admitted that in addition to keeping people connected, "Facebook turns human beings into brands."

I think what we really crave, more than ten thousand mouths singing our praises, is intimacy.

Steve Carrell, superstar of The Office, The 40-Year-Old Virgin, and dozens of other films, once said that his favorite part of any Hollywood award ceremony is eating a hamburger with his wife after the big event. He realized the love and affection of one person is more significant than the celebration of millions of strangers.

I just Googled the roots of the word 'intimate,' and what I found is worth mentioning here. It comes from the Latin word *intimus*, which means 'inmost, innermost, or deepest.' We want the deepest parts of ourselves to be known, but we can only express our superficial elements online. We put so much thought and effort into our online profiles and relationships then wonder why we still feel alone and unsatisfied. We are hungry for intimacy.

The reason I started this chapter with my story about briefly being famous is simple: Most of us, when we sign in to our social media accounts, are subconsciously looking for some kind of fame. We probably won't admit it out loud and we may not even realize it ourselves.

But after each Instagram post, how often do you slip your phone out of your pocket to check the number of likes it earned? We feel just a little more satisfied when a post ignites a conversation and warrants dozens of comments. Big moments like graduations and wedding days are guaranteed to rake in heaps of attention, as are photogenic vacations featuring suntanned bikini bodies.

Truth be told, I secretly used to anticipate my engagement just to see how many likes it would earn. *Surely that will be my record-setting day for internet acclaim and congratulation,* I told myself, and I know I'm not alone.

Humans have this innate desire to be seen and recognized.

In some small way, I feel like I have 'gone up to the mountain and come back down,' and can tell you that it's lonely at the top. I have had millions of views worldwide, and I can tell you it's not all it's cracked up to be. Being digitally acclaimed but socially disconnected is a sad and cold way to go through life. Striving for all that attention is exhausting, and when it comes, it's not very fulfilling.

You just want more.

In a survey I gave at Wheat Ridge High School one junior named Connor wrote, "I look at social media whenever I feel lonely. And then I feel lonely because of it. It shows us everyone else's peaks and allows us to compare it to our valleys."

I bet if we paused and thought logically for a moment, we would realize something. We are all well aware by now that everyone posts their 'best self' to social media. We tend to untag photos where we look like we're about to sneeze, or when our vibe seems off. We don't post pictures of ourselves watching Netflix, getting ready for bed, or anything else that would make our lives seem drab or otherwise ordinary.

Yet what do we typically do with those we are closest to? Watch Netflix, get ready for bed, and the other boring and ordinary parts of life. We live life *together*. All of it, not just the exciting parts.

Imagine spending a day with someone who would only let you look at one side of their face—their better side. They would sit in the brunch restaurant at an angle, so the light hit their cheekbones just right. They *only* walked on your right side so you couldn't see their bad side. This person is so concerned with never appearing ugly for a second that they are constantly looking in their phone camera and their reflection in passing windows in order to check everything.

It would be horrendous!

Yet this is what we tend to do with our online profiles. We only let the world see our best side as we painstakingly curate and doctor ourselves to appear as untarnished and pristine as possible.

In 2005 Duke University conducted a study on 'monkey celebrities.' The results help explain this craving all of us have for fame and associating ourselves with powerful people.

In the experiment, the monkeys were seated before a couple screens, each playing slideshows of monkeys from their twelve member troop. Depending on which screen the monkeys paid attention to, they would receive a squirt of cherry juice—their favorite drink. What the scientists found is that monkeys were willing to sacrifice some of their juice in order to look longer at the alpha monkeys from their troop. They received 10% *less* juice as the 'price' of looking at these stronger monkeys.

On the opposite end, the monkeys needed to be 'paid' 5% *more* juice in order to look at pictures of lower-ranking monkeys. Some of them preferred to look at the gray square which preceded the images than look at the more subordinate monkeys.

The experiment was conducted to study similarities between humans and their nearest biological relatives, and examine how similar the two were when it came to prominence. The results were conclusive that, just like humans, monkeys are willing to pay to look at images of their own celebrities. Dr. Glimcher, one of the lead scientists, explained, "People are willing to pay money to look at pictures of high-ranking humans. When you fork out $3" for a celebrity gossip magazine, "you're doing exactly what the monkeys are doing. "The difference between this study and People magazine," he said, "is that the monkeys actually know the individuals in the picture."

Which brings us back to social media.

We spend cumulative days of our lives staring at the more beautiful and interesting people of Facebook and Instagram, and almost none on those whom we decide are less important or attractive. More than any other time in history, we have the technology to decisively indicate who is more worthy of our attention. Just look at who has more followers on any branch of social media: Beautiful people or less attractive ones? The platforms have become grounds on which to base your worth and value in society; all you need to do is take a quick glance at someone's follower count and monitor how many likes they regularly receive. Most of us are quick to talk about how stupid or reckless all these celebrities are, yet subtly leave out the fact that they are all undeniably attractive compared to the average person.

When we base our value on how well we perform on social media, we are fighting a losing battle. We're the Sisyphus endlessly pushing uphill the boulder of our own importance and fame.

Of course, social media has its benefits. I have friends I've met around the world, and the fact that I get to peer into their lives from time to time is pretty neat. But when I'm honest—and I would bet when you are as well—it has become so much more all-consuming than that. It's not simply a phonebook to keep in touch with pals, it is a stage. It's the largest stage in the world, where we are beckoned to come and present ourselves, testing who can stand up to the scrutiny of the harsh internet.

Some of you will pass with higher ratings than others. But what good is that? What benefits are legitimately added to your life when you break that 50-Like goal? Or 100? Or 1,000?

I can tell you the numbers are never enough. I remember years ago, longing to break 50 Likes on an Instagram picture. *Because THEN I will feel appreciated. THEN I will be like the cooler kids who earn 50 Likes on the daily!*

Months later, I passed 50. In fact, I passed 500 and even 500,000.

I broke 5 million views,

and the longing for more still remained. Instead of looking at fellow college students, I began comparing myself to the likes of Justin Bieber and Terry Crews, who rake in millions of Likes daily. You will never reach a certain amount of Likes that will satiate your craving.

The numbers never add up.

You may be a reader who says *But Ethan, that's not me! I just post on Facebook for fun, for my friends and family! I don't really care how many likes I get.* The truth is, there is that fraction of a percent about whom this is true (and I envy you). But I encourage you to ask yourself, *why* do you post anything on Facebook, Instagram, et al? What is your purpose behind sharing selfies, clever quotes, or even spiritual insights?

Perhaps the most subtle tool of spiritual distraction is the very thing we think is so great about social media. I often catch myself conjuring some clever quip about Jesus or the nature of God's love, and rather than dwelling on it and applying it to my own life, I rapidly heave it onto the internet. Maybe God wanted to just teach me something, but in favor of publicity, I threw that little spiritual nugget on Twitter…to get Likes.

It's scary to realize we live in a culture where someone could give out endless truths about God online and yet have no actual relationship with Him. We may be able to dish out scripture after scripture, but what good is it if we cannot sit alone quietly in a room with our Creator? With the One who loves us deeply and fiercely?

No amount of media attention or social media followers can ultimately fill this void within us to be known, loved and appreciated. Over the course of its narrative arc, the Bible continually reinforces the nearness of God to His people.

He is the husband and we are the wife.

He is the Father and we are the sons and daughters.

He is the Shepherd who intimately knows us, the sheep.

No amount of Insta-fame could rival this kind of intimate knowledge. Our souls pine to be known in ways that cannot be conveyed through filtered photographs or social media profiles.

As Johnny Lee would sing, perhaps our recurring feelings of loneliness cloud us because we are 'looking for [intimacy] in all the wrong places.' We look to social media to accommodate a longing whose weight it cannot bear. To be known intimately means revealing our ugly sides as well as the beautiful ones.

Pastor Tim Keller argues that this deep longing to be known and appreciated arises because no one on earth is 'big' enough to satisfy our need for approval, not even the collective praise of the masses. He preached in a sermon once,

"We want someone of ultimate glory loving us. Not just love in general. What we need is this ultimate assurance of who we are, ultimate assurance of our worth. We need someone like *that* loving us like *that*. We need someone we think the world of thinking the world of us. We need the praise of the praiseworthy."

I know some people who seriously freak out if a celebrity follows them online or likes one of their pictures. They have attributed to this person more 'weight,' or significance than the average person. It's a dangerous thing to give a human more magnitude than they are due, yet there is a reason we perpetually fall into this mindset. We're programmed to worship. It has to do with what Keller mentioned: desiring the praise of the praiseworthy. We are so quick to forget that Jesus—the most praiseworthy of all—has this fiery love for each one of us.

He desires you.

He is attracted to you.

When we realize that God—the only One large enough to quell our need for love and attention—is intimately aware of our lives, of our needs and wants, our insecurities and accomplishments, then all human accolades fade in comparison. The Maker of all things thinks that we're pretty cool, so why should we care if a few tweens double tap our picture? Keeping things in this perspective will help unbend our hearts from years of being programmed to chase after attention.

YOU LOOK COOLER ONLINE

"I always knew that I'd love you from afar..."
-Vance Joy, *From Afar*

"Do you want to marry me?" she lowered her eyes and smirked as she asked me the question.

My brain quickly scanned my rolodex of sly, flirty responses.

"I'm not sure yet," I answered. "Ask me after dinner."

I was sitting in a bamboo sushi hut somewhere outside of Los Angeles with a fashion designer. I had come across her Instagram profile some weeks before through some mutual friends and started up a conversation. I was living in Chicago at the time and had taken a trip all the way to the West Coast to meet her.

Within two months I had made two trips to California to meet her, and toward the end of the second trip it was becoming clear that we didn't have much in common. She had a clear direction in which her life was moving. I had neither direction nor forward motion.

Our relationship began and ended online.

We exchanged plenty of long-distance phone calls and Skype conversations. It was clear that we were hovering in that area between relationship and friendship for a few months, but we both felt like it just wasn't right. Like one of those socks with a big lump on the side of the toe. Like there was something in between us, aside from 1578 miles of highway.

We non-committal Millennials call this the "talking" phase.

Years later, I was getting off work at 8pm. During my shift, a ravishing girl had friend requested me on Facebook and it turned out she was staying two hours away outside San Diego for the weekend. I had a dilemma: Drive for two hours, get there at ten at night, and risk wasting 4 hours worth of gas; or not take the risk, play it safe, and miss an opportunity to meet a new lover? I also had to wake up at 7am the next day.

I made up my mind and told my roommate that I had to drive to San Diego.

"Why?" He asked.

I employed my favorite line from *Good Will Hunting*, "I gotta go see about a girl," and was out the door.

Two hours later I met her at the home where she was staying. She was even prettier in person. I discovered she had never been to In-N-Out, so we had a late night burger and then drove around Escondido, the mountainous town she was visiting.

At eleven, I drove us across the serpentine road that slithered through the valleys of the region. I told her I liked her as we curved around the hem of one of the hills. The air was silent in my car, save some acoustic song which crooned through the speakers in the background.

Then she told me she liked me too.

By midnight we were lying on a blanket in a field, stargazing and talking.

I touched her hand.

By 2am she was tired and I dropped her off at the house, then began the trek back to Los Angeles. You can do the math: I didn't get much sleep that night.

The next night I had decided to make the trip south once again and spend the last few hours of her visit with her. We crammed a month's worth of romance into the following morning, driving all over San Diego and sightseeing. We ate croissants in a cafe while the sun rose and I photographed her in the mountains. We read each other poetry in a bookstore.

Then I took her to the airport and watched her vanish through the sliding glass doors pulling her carry-on behind her.

Our two days of romance evaporated almost as quickly as they had rushed in. We both tried to hold onto this new chance at romance, but once again, it just didn't fit right. Like most clothes at a thrift store.

We both had this idealized version of the other, generated by our respective Facebook pictures, without any real knowledge of the other. As we got to know each other over the next couple weeks, we found that we weren't as perfect as we had imagined each other to be.

Social media had flummoxed us once again.

I'm embarrassed to admit that I have about a half dozen of these stories. I can outline them like this:

    I.   See attractive person on social media
    II. Initiate contact (choose two)
        1. Poke
        2. Comment on picture
        3. Friend Request
        4. Message
    III. Begin conversation
        1. Explain why I contacted them out of the blue
        2. Sound more interesting than I am
    IV. Arrange a meeting in person and meet.
        1. Dress cool
        2. Walk up casually eating an apple or something cool like that
        3. Talk and get to know each other
        4. Act cool
    V. Over time, realize we're not the people we pretended to be on social media
    VI. Conclude relationship

I'm pretty sure I'm not the only one who's ever done this. In fact, I would wager most of us have similar outlines for relationships born digitally.

I don't need to waste words talking about how we are all very different people online than we are in person. Or how each of us tends to put our best version of our life on Facebook and hide the boring or unattractive bits. Or point out that nearly no one's life looks as cool as their online presence makes it appear.

Instead, I want to focus on the effects of these facts.

Of course, the first and foremost of these is loneliness. Envy and jealously often get blended in as well, and maybe a dash of shame as we see people whose lives seem so much more photogenic and adventurous than our own.

Social media was invented as a way of connecting people, but more than anything, as Web 2.0 relentlessly stormed our lives, it has built walls between us.

Think about your closest friends, the ones you see in person daily. Classmates, family members, best friends or dorm buddies. I would wager that if you looked at any of their social media accounts, the person presented there is slightly different than the person you know in reality, to varying degrees of course. It is nearly impossible to represent oneself to 100% accuracy online. Each of us carefully curates and maintains the presence we have on the internet, sometimes to the extent that we present someone else entirely.

Our online persona is a heavily filtered one.

Brennan Manning wrote extensively on the notion of *the impostor*—someone we create within ourselves who is cooler, stronger, and better than we are, and whom we send out into the world to hide our true selves. In other words, she is the best version of yourself which the public sees. The impostor typically originates when we are young, after being hurt or being made to feel weak. In his book *Abba's Child*, Manning writes:

> While the impostor draws his identity from past achievements and the adulation of others, the true self claims identity in its belovedness. We encounter God in the ordinariness of life: not in the search for spiritual highs and extraordinary, mystical experiences but in our simple presence in life.

If the Impostor inside each of us is a flame trying to eat away at our souls, social media is gasoline being dumped on the fire, causing it to roar into an untamable blaze. For many of us, posting to social media is a hunt for Likes and encouraging comments. There is no room for weakness in our digital Impostors. No one can see the ugly side of us.

I gave a friend a hard time recently when he shared a picture on Instagram and deleted it a few hours later when it only earned three Likes.

The majority of our lives would earn less than three Likes.

We don't share life online, we share highlights.

This has led to a culture of people trying to fake it, like a puppeteer hiding themselves behind a curtain and pulling the strings to bring their pristine online puppets to life. Younger generations, those who entered high school after the social media craze had swept the world, don't even know life apart from the internet. In my surveys, even among seventh graders, it was rare to find a student who was *not* on social media. To many of them, digital acclaim and popularity is the measure of their worth.

I shared those two stories in the beginning of the chapter to show just how different we are from our online personas. My best friendships and richest romantic relationships did not start or grow online. They started with time together. They started with inside jokes and long conversations in the backyard.

I rarely ever look at my close friends' Facebook profiles because I'm already familiar with their lives. I know what they're up to and what they look like. The people I 'stalk' the most are people I am *not* close with; people who are far away, or strangers. Former flames or potential sweethearts.

I think many of us are lonely because we put more effort into our digital relationships than our tangible ones. For some reason, having a lot of followers and showering in Likes seem to be higher on some of our priority lists than spending quality time with friends, away from technology. I can even think of times I've gotten together with friends to go on an adventure purely to take pictures to put on Instagram. Who are we trying to impress? Strangers?

I see social media starving many of the *real* relationships in my life, and of course, when relationships are starved, loneliness dives in. Our New Loneliness does not come from a lack of connectivity or access to people; it comes from an abundance of shallow relationships and superficial noise. When this noise is removed and our phones die and we are left in silence, we recognize this lack of depth intensely.

In my pastor's sermon last night, he talked about meeting with a man who was feeling distant from God. "I could see the real, six-foot version of him sitting there before me," he explained. "But I could also see this little two-inch version of himself darting around inside his body. He was so anxious as he ran this way and that and could not just be still. He did not have peace within himself." This is such a good description of the New Loneliness.

It's a miniature version of ourselves that can't sit still and doesn't want direct attention. And it's very, very busy impressing people.

I think what we often identify as 'loneliness' is really unrest and a lack of peace which is normally drowned out by a digital din. Then when we are truly alone and in quiet, this void rises to the forefront of our minds. Because it only happens when we are alone, we mistake it for loneliness. I mean...

how many times have you looked at your phone since you started this chapter?

Take this quiz and see how well you did!
(Answers at the end of chapter)

A. None

B. 1-2 times

C. 3-5 times

D. 5+ times

What we need is not more followers, but deeper friendships—something social media will never help us to achieve.

One 2014 study found that people who consider themselves 'lonely' are far more likely to publicly divulge more personal information on their Facebook profiles. People who did not identify as lonely were more likely to keep this information about themselves private, reserved only for their friends and family. The leader of the study was unsurprised however, and commented, "It makes sense that the people who felt lonely would disclose this type of information. They want to make it easier for others to initiate contact with them, which may help them overcome their feelings of loneliness."

The irony here is that social media does very little to take away our loneliness, and even contributes to making it worse. When we turn to screens in order to alleviate our loneliness, we should not be surprised when the two-dimensional world fails to satiate our hunger for intimacy.

My friend Dalton cracks me up because he will often launch into a diatribe about how online, everyone is just data. "Everyone is data! Every picture is data! Every comment is data! Every time I send something off into the internet, it's just...*data!*

I laugh every time I see his Instagram or Facebook bio, which simply reads: 'data.' Occasionally he changes it to "Generic human being.' He recognized that everyone can make themselves look any way they want online, and it's all just data; nothing human about it. The internet offers us a malleable version of ourselves which we can mold and present exactly how we want.

To a large degree, Dalton is correct. Of course, you can glean a little information off of someone's online profile, but to engage in a relationship purely based on digital *data* is crazy. We are made for human contact, not romance with ones and zeros. Binary codes have no warmth or emotions. They cannot hold you as you weep. They are static while humans are constantly in flux. We are a dynamic people, growing and learning and sinking into depression and climbing mountains. To engage with only a fraction of a person's humanity—their data—is to dehumanize one another.

We were made for whole relationships with one another, yet if we examined the amount of time we spend searching for this online, we would probably be ashamed of how much effort we pour into digital connection.

If you ever want to get spooked, read some essays by Tristan Harris or BJ Fogg. They have spent years of their lives studying companies such as Facebook, Snapchat, and Google, and how these titans of the industry program our brains to crave their products.

Look at it this way: Facebook (and all of these companies) earn more money the more time you spend on their website or app. Therefore, they are going to do everything in their power to keep you on their app—and keep you coming back to it—as often and for as long as possible.

Let's look at just two examples, pulled from Harris' essay *How Technology Hijacks People's Minds — from a Magician and Google's Design Ethicist*, an excellent read to sum up just how social media companies take advantage of our brains.

Social reciprocity is a fancy way of saying that when one person does an action to us, we feel inclined to response in like. If someone says "Thank you," we are inclined to say "You're welcome." If someone messages us, we are inclined to message them back.

> It's in [these companies'] interests to heighten the feeling of urgency and social reciprocity. For example, Facebook automatically tells the sender when you "saw" their message, instead of letting you avoid disclosing whether you read it ("now that you *know* I've seen the message, I *feel even more obligated* to respond.") By contrast, Apple more respectfully lets users toggle "Read Receipts" on or off.

These small features of various apps are not a mere accident. They are carefully constructed to keep us on their platform for as long and as often as possible.

Another method of commandeering our brains is via the human quest for social approval. Remember how creepy it was when Facebook first started recognizing faces in photographs? It suggests a friend to tag in the picture, and it is scarily accurate. This is no accident, nor is it for the convenience of us, the users. Writes Harris, "Facebook uses automatic suggestions like this to get people to tag more people, creating more social externalities and interruptions." He also notes that we are most vulnerable when a new picture of us is uploaded, especially by other people, so companies try to prey on this as much as possible.

Each of us wants to be approved and appreciated by those we love, so the more Facebook can coax us to tag others in photos, the more it can create a sort of 'spiral of events,' which sucks more people back to their phones or laptops through one simple action.

Now, why would I spend so much time critiquing social media and its use of our brain chemistry? Because many of us still think that social media is just that—social. And by constantly staying connected to our social media, we are staying in touch with our loved ones.

In reality, we are simply playing into the hand of these gargantuan companies; doing exactly what they want by whipping our phones out every other minute to check something.

What we are *not* doing is connecting to our friends and family in deep and meaningful ways. Understanding how these companies work should make it slightly easier to unplug or disconnect more often. I'm not saying we should all delete our profiles and live in the woods, but I think we should begin to be aware of how we use social media versus how social media uses us.

Spend some time thinking about what aspects of social media are truly beneficial—for instance, messaging friends who live across the Atlantic—and which parts have laid siege to your behavior patterns, taking you away from the present moment dozens, if not hundreds, of times a day. Try switching off your phone notifications and limiting the number of times you check your accounts in a week.

We can reprogram our brains away from those tiny red boxes alerting us once again to our value.

There's this 8mm film reel that plays in my mind when I cast my vision back to the summer of 2007: Lila and I are racing down the train tracks which cut through Cape Cod's greenery to the old wooden playground a mile from her house.

I see her arms sway up and to the right as she tries to maintain balance on one of the rails. Then we jump from one wooden beam to the next. Some days, as we cut through this railway, the slow train would roll by and we would stand near the bushes and watch it chug past.

I see us many midnights ago swimming beneath the meteor shower at the Barnstable Yacht Club. In the summer, the waters of the Atlantic are illuminated by the phosphorescence, tiny organisms that light up in the water when they are agitated. When you paddle your hand through the water, they momentarily light up and streak through the brackish ripples. As we swam off the dock of the ancient yacht club, stars were shooting in the sky above us and in the water below us.

Gravity flipped upside down.

That summer we lay in fields and looked at the bright blue sky, so painfully beautiful despite the singularity of its hue. We swam in many of the Cape's hundreds of ponds. On the gray days we curled up in the blankets of her living room and watched independent films.

We were the dearest of friends.

It wasn't until Lila went back to boarding school on Long Island in the fall that we realized the feelings we had developed for one another.

We exchanged letters ornamented with doodles, folded over pressed flowers. Winter rolled into the northeast as our love began to grow just in time to keep us warm. There was the night in October when I surprised her in New York and we held hands for the first time in the back seat of her parent's van. We were sneaky. Holding those five white fingers seemed like smuggling rubies out of the Louvre.

She would return to Cape Cod for the occasional weekend visit and I remember spending many of those days with her, wrapped in a blanket watching the gray-green waves crash against the snowy shore. Smoke came out our mouths as we exhaled soft words for each other while we sat on the coast, wrapped up and intertwined.

Lila and I shared everything. Every song we heard had echoes of the other, as did every poem and film. Each snowflake that fell seemed to whisper some new form of beauty which we couldn't wait to wrap into a letter and send to the other.

There was no time like it.

This rich season of romance and beauty came to a screeching halt when my father announced one evening that we would be moving to Colorado. Lila and I were already maintaining a long-distance relationship, but the three hour drive seemed much more palatable than a 30-hour cross country expedition.

My first few months back in the West were hard, as the girl I loved was on the far side of the country, lonely beneath the overcast Long Island sky.

We slowly drifted apart over the early months of 2008, and by the next summer our relationship was little more than a basketful of memories we would often dig our hands into for warmth.

The richest relationship of my life had ended.

Even now, almost a decade later, I look on that time with such tender fondness. There was nothing digital about my relationship with Lila. It was alive and organic as the veiny leaves of the oak leaves surrounding us that June. Incidentally, it was during that time I first created a social media account, so the entire concept was still somewhat alien to me. Facebook was fun and exciting, but certainly not all-consuming. I had only received my first flip phone a few months prior, and the notion of smartphones—carrying the World Wide Web in your pocket—was still a few years away.

Our relationship was so beautiful and intimate because no part of it was constructed from online presentation. We knew each other from church, and long before Facebook flooded our lives, we had a personal knowledge of each other. Lila and I were close to each other in the tangible, real, human sense.

I think the social media revolution has happened so slowly that few of us even noticed. Now, when we meet someone in person, we rush to look them up online. Rather than engage in personal, meaningful conversation, we investigate their *data*. We forsake good eye contact and dialogue in favor of checking out their two-dimensional production.

In preparing for this book, I have explained the concept countless times. "We are lonely not because of a lack of connectivity, but because of a lack of depth, and blah blah blah..." The first thing out of everyone's mouth is something about technology and social media causing this. I explain that yes, that's part of it, but not all of it. People are not unaware of how technology has separated us and created strangers out of roommates.

The problem most of us face, then, is what to do about it. When people ask me what the cure is for loneliness, I tell them with a very straight face:

'Delete all your social media accounts.'

Small shockwaves of terror consume them as they consider the possibility of a life disconnected from the world, so they think. Most of us have friends who have intentionally cut themselves off from social media. They seem to have a peace and patience within them which most of us lack. They aren't hungry for digital attention, nor do they expend energy constructing an online presence.

They really aren't missing out on much.

They may not be quite as up to date on the latest memes, and they've probably missed several heated political arguments. But for what cost? They are more present in the moment and are able to connect to the people in front of them more deeply than those of us fretting about our latest post.

For many of us, deleting all of our social media is not really an option. I have found it very relaxing to limit my intake of social media. I have none on my phone, so I can only check it on my laptop. Initially, it may seem scary to delete those little App squares from your phone. It feels like letting go of a good friend, or maybe even ripping out the IV delivering sweet nutrients to your body.

Try it for a week.

Reduce your social media presence and see if the noise and hype generated by all the updates begins to fade away. Watch your blood pressure go down.

We were not made to be crammed into 1's and 0's and displayed in binary online. We were made for intimate and dynamic relationships with other humans.

Humans.

With skin and bones and soft necks and weird smells. If social media is getting in the way of you and your friends, try taking a break from it. See how much richer it is to interact with people face-to-face, rather than screen-to-screen.

Score key:

A. Congratulations, you fall into one of three categories. Either you were born before the Revolutionary War; You have been stranded on a small island in the Galapagos for the past three decades and swam back to the mainland just to purchase this book; or you have achieved a level of peace and presence rivaled only by philosophical giants such as Mother Teresa, King David, and Winnie the Pooh.

B. Average college student score. You were born before the age of cell phones and Internet 2.0, so you know how to cope without electronics cemented to your palm, but still have to stay up to date. With a little work, you could be on your way to some pretty good meditation and maybe even human levitation!

C. Hard to say; this one could go either way. Either you're still in high school or you're one of those grandparents who got hooked on social media and frequently misuses inappropriate emojis. Nothing wrong with a little distraction, but let's work to get that score to an A or B, okay?

D. Seek help. Regardless of your age, gender, and income, your family misses you. Your friends miss you. They want you to come back from screenland. It's been so long since they've seen your pupils. Do you remember what they look like? You keep telling them you're fine and you can quit any time, but one day you'll walk into your house and they'll all be sitting in a semi-circle with handwritten letters in their laps. You would benefit from finding the largest stone you can lift, setting your phone on the ground, and dropping the stone on your phone. Do it thrice for good measure. You will have withdrawal headaches, but you will survive. #stonethephone

GOD IS NOT A HIPSTER

"There are nearly seven billion people in the world. None of those people is an extra. They're all the leads of their own stories."
-Synecdoche New York

I once went to a New Year's Eve party at the home of a Greek family. It was simultaneously awkward and awesome to dance with a few dozen strangers, the children to the grandparents all dancing in one big circle. A few of the women were teaching us the steps and I sloppily tried to keep up. Both my palms were pressed flat against the hands on either side of me like a high five that got stuck, and we were *step-step-squat-kick-stepping* to the traditional Greek music.

It was a unique experience to not only see seniors and kindergarteners dancing in the same circle, but doing the exact same moves. There was a unity in the group that was somewhat foreign to me, an individualistic American who was used to solo club dancing, and there was something beautiful about it.

As I looked into the history of dance, I realized that it is one of the most fitting ways to describe the culture in which we currently find ourselves. Just like the circle at the home of the Greek family, dance originated in tribal and communal circles. It reflected a unity within the group as the members all mirrored one another's steps and embodied their culture and their bonds to one another.

Over time, the familial dances began to fragment into smaller groups as ballroom dancing and other dances involving partners overtook the west. No longer did children need to mimic their parents' moves, but they could jump on the floor with their sweetheart. Now duos swept one another across the floorboards in rhythmic flutters like two butterflies tied together. The groups were now smaller, but there was still some form of symmetry to their steps.

In the past 100 years however, dancing has regressed to the opposite extreme of communal or tribal movement. In the *Encyclopedia of American Studies*, Luke C. Kahlich notes:

> Dance, like all forms of cultural expression, reflects the society in which it exists. Since the early 1920s, new freedom in what body parts to move and how to move them have mirrored changes in social values and attitudes toward the body...The Harlem Renaissance brought the range of African American dances such as the lindy and jitterbug into the mainstream. The energetic partner dances of the 1930s and 1940s sought to escape from the Great Depression and World War II. As these threats faded, dances became more individualistic, with rock and roll and dances such as the twist of the 1960s and later freestyle dances such as the frug and the jerk. Disco dancing of the 1970s and street-based dances of the 1980s (breakdancing, punk, raves, hip-hop) merged to form the social dances of the 1990s, incorporating both a personal style and a strong influence from the African-based hip-hop style.

Kahlich specifically points out just how certain dance styles reflected the larger cultural backdrop against which it was set. While older forms of dancing such as swing or square dance are still very much alive, the prevailing form of dance in America is a free-for-all club experience with no predetermined rhythm or flow, but a hectic and chaotic synecdoche of our individualistic society. As Western culture has become more and more individualistic, so has our style of dancing left behind the more collectivistic in favor of the solo. Everything is personalized. Everyone is special to the point that no one is really special anymore.

Everyone gets an award.

Over the centuries, as we departed our tribal and communal roots and moved toward this individualized culture, people drifted apart. Now you're only worthy if you can prove your worth, whereas before, you were valuable because you were a part of a community.

For some reason, it's hard to picture an ancient Native American teenager complaining about feeling alone in a crowded wigwam.

It just doesn't fit.

Theirs is a beautiful culture of togetherness and family, but there is something unique about western cultures that have created this space for us to be alone while in the midst of others. As our styles of dance reflect, we have moved more out of sync with others and onto a floor where everyone is doing their own thing.

In some sense, this cultural shift from unity to uniqueness has created far more room than ever before for us to be lonely. When the focus of a culture is a tribe, community, or family, less emphasis is on the individual, which pulls the culture away from things like insecurity, defense mechanisms, and of course, loneliness.

Even in the past couple decades, there has been a marked decrease in communal engagement. Robert D. Putnam records this in depth in his book *Bowling Alone: The Collapse and Revival of American Community*. Just as a dollar bill has Financial Capital, and a hammer has Physical Capital because of its usefulness, cultures develop Social Capital, which measures the interconnectedness of the citizens. Putnam observes that America has shifted from a culture of communities—having a high Social Capital—to a more individualistic, or lonely culture. We have put less value in gathering together. Bridge groups, activist organizations, sports clubs, and community events are in decline from where they were half a century ago.

Robert Bellah, esteemed sociology professor and author, put the cultural condition succinctly. He wrote,

> There is a very big problem, and its solution is hard to envision. Just when we are moving to an ever greater validation of the sacredness of the individual person, our capacity to imagine a social fabric that would hold individuals together is vanishing… the sacredness of the individual is not balanced by any sense of the whole or concern for the common good.

For those of us who speak English, he said that America is becoming more focused on individual identity, and as a result, the social groups and unity which once was so strong is crumbling. I think the use of the word *fabric* here is perfect: If each of us is one thread in a much larger tapestry, we are meant to be woven together and intersect in each others' lives. What our culture is doing, however, is pulling it apart in order to focus on each individual thread and proclaim, "YOU are special! YOU are special! And YOU are special," to the degree that we no longer resemble a beautiful tapestry, but a heap of threads strewn about the floor.

Our emphasis on the individual has pulled us apart more than it has drawn us together. We need to learn to see ourselves as part of a bigger picture instead of focusing so heavily on ourselves.

I recently met someone who moved from Chicago to Denver a few months ago, and his reason for the transition was interesting. He had been very involved in Chicago's restaurant scene for several years. Chicago, set right in the center of America's farm country, has a myriad of world-renowned restaurants. People make trips to the metropolis just for some of the city's culinary experiences.

My new friend explained that the reason for this is not just its prime agricultural location, but many of the people in Chicago's food industry have a unified vision. They all want to push the boundaries for what can be done when it comes to food, and they also have a desire to make Chicago a better city.

They are brought together by a sense of healthy competition.

In Denver, however, he described the scene differently. Colorado's restaurants tend to be more inwardly focused. They want what's best for their own eateries more than what's best for their city as a whole. As a result, Denver has *not* become a staple city in the food business and many of the restaurants remain static and unchallenged in their culinary innovations.

My friend wants to bring a spirit of unity to Denver. He wants them to interact with one another, as he saw the restaurants in Chicago doing, in order to push one another to be better.

I thought this comparison between the two cities was fascinating, as it reflects so much about the American society as a whole. When we are united by a common vision, as well as a competition which pushes us to be better, we thrive. We win awards and become renowned for pushing back boundaries. Yet when we prefer to stay unchallenged and focus only on ourselves, we stagnate, don't move forward, and grow lonely.

I think much of Christian growth—including moving out of loneliness and into intimacy—involves inviting others into our lives in a meaningful way. Not inviting them over just to play video games, but inviting them into our thoughts, emotions, struggles, and so on.

Inviting them to challenge us.

By being connected, we thrive, but in doing everything alone, we suffer.

In our post-everything culture, there is one stereotype that has risen to reflect the attitude of our society as a whole.

The hipster.

It may be odd to think of hipsters as defining a society they try so hard to critique, but over the past decade or two, hipsterdom has laid siege to the American population, whether we know it or not. We have become a country defined by our opinions more than our beliefs or actions. We prefer to laugh at things rather than change them. Why this shift? Why now?

April 20, 1999. Two teenagers walked into Columbine High School in Littleton, Colorado and began open firing on the students and teachers. Thirteen people were killed, fifteen if you count the suicides of the gunmen. I was two miles away at the time.

September 11, 2001. Two planes were pirated and slammed into the World Trade Center in New York City. 2,871 people died. A third plane hit part of the Pentagon, killing 125. The following week, comedy show hosts David Letterman and Jon Stewart wept before their cameras on live television.

Because there are some things you can't write jokes about.

Until you can.

Fifteen years later, we have learned how to satirize even the heavier parts of life. I hear jokes about Saddam Hussein, Hitler, and now ISIS. In a kingdom of hipsters, irony reigns supreme and when someone tries to take something seriously, they become the next target.

Let me back up a little bit and define what exactly defines this notorious subculture.

In his 2012 article *The Hipster in All of Us*, Mike Cosper writes that hipsters are marked by their "sneer of cynicism. Their core value is irony, and the aesthetic they embrace—their posture towards the culture around them—is defined by a sense of cynical superiority over it." Essentially, the hipster is someone who is *in*. And if you're not in, then you're out. If you stand for something—anything—you become the butt of the joke.

Rather than stand for something, the hipster tends to identify himself as one who is opposed to everything. Or at least, he is making fun of everything. And in this biting ironic identity, hipsters have found a way to "hide in public" behind a wall of outwardly-pointing fingers.

I've been describing hipsters in the third person, but I need to remember that to some degree, I am a hipster. You are a hipster. Each of us has things we are not comfortable talking about, or things we make fun of because we don't know how to react.

We each have our own ways of hiding in public.

Hipsters emerged a few generations ago in response to the shiny archetype of the American dream. They denied that the nice house, white fence, and two-point-four kids were the only way to live a successful life, so they created their own as a response: The rebel without a cause. Today, however, the hipster is a revolutionary against nothing in particular because they stand for nothing in particular.

By hiding behind humor and irony, the hipster is essentially bulletproof. Cosper writes, "One who mocks the hipster only affirms the hipster's self-important superiority. By mocking mustaches, skinny jeans, and vintage bicycles, you reveal yourself as an outsider; you're not in on the joke."

As the popularity of an ironic lifestyle rose, so did our ability to keep up with surface-level conversation and jokes. No longer do we want to sit around and discuss philosophy or theology; now we prefer to quote Nacho Libre or make innocent jabs at one another. Humor is king, and when humor is king, the one who tries to be serious is the new misfit.

The jester has taken his crown.

Matt Ashby wrote for *Salon* about the rise and danger of irony in a culture:

> At one time, irony served to challenge the establishment; now it is the establishment. The art of irony has turned into ironic art. Irony for irony's sake. A smart aleck making bomb noises in front of a city in ruins. But irony without a purpose enables cynicism. It stops at disavowal and destruction, fearing strong conviction is a mark of simplicity and delusion.

A billion factors led to the rise of our new "hipster culture," but I think some of them are more obvious than others. As society shifted from tribes and communities to individualized capitalistic institutions, people were suddenly left alone to scramble for their own identities. Christians have church; Muslims have Mosque; and Jews have temple. But what about the rising secular populace? In what do they root their identity?

It's easier to sarcastically criticize established communities than found a new one, so this rootless generation learned to avoid confronting their lack of foundation and opted toward comedy and satire.

Especially after events like Columbine and 9/11, we are left wondering how to react. Pray? No, that's too exclusive. Weep? That's too vulnerable.

So we make jokes.

No one can make fun of the person telling the jokes because laughter is the whole point.

When Letterman wept on live TV, something shifted. America squirmed in their couch cushions. Why is this comedian—someone we pay to make us laugh—crying before his audience?

Humor is easier.

Hitler killed 6 million Jews and the best form of homage we can give them is a joke about a pizza screaming in the oven.

We've forgotten how to grieve.

In the film *Funny People,* Adam Sandler plays a famous comedian who has been diagnosed with a terminal disease. Many parts of the film are painful to watch as he attempts to maintain the facade of one of the funniest people alive while simultaneously dealing with his imminent mortality. Near the end of the film, as more people learn about his illness, Sandler explodes, "Am I not allowed to be happy or something? I've been living alone and alone and alone. That's my life. This is the only girl I've ever loved and I'm not supposed to do anything about this? When am I supposed to be happy? Why does everyone else get to be happy?"

When our lives, like that of Sandler's character, are built only on humor, it's next to impossible to look into the face of death and know how to react. How do you talk about cancer if you're a comedian? How do you tell your family you deeply love them through a shtick?

If our lives and identities are built on the volatile foundation of how many laughs we can coax out of people, any subject of depth will make us uncomfortable. It is a great defense mechanism because it is attractive;

people like funny people.

But it is also dangerous when we find ourselves unable to engage in serious conversation because we're scared of what lies beneath the surface of our own veneer. Hipster culture has largely contributed to our becoming the New Lonely; strangers in our own skin, unable to be alone for the lack of peace that ensues. We can't face ourselves in silence because we don't even know what we stand for. Our personalities tend to be coated in a thick membrane of irony. One that disguises our real imperfections, feelings, and struggles. One that minimizes our real thoughts and insecurities.

Learning how to break out of this membrane—this second skin which hides our real, raw, vulnerable selves takes effort. If you're someone who

.de behind humor and jokes, try to be intentional about having
sional deep conversation. I'm not against humor or jokes at all.

eaking hilarious.

But I also think it's important to dive below the superficial and shallow
depths of humor for the good of our souls and our personhood. When I
was at my third college in Chicago, I had a standing meeting every Friday
at 6:30am with a friend. I remember many wintry mornings, plodding that
fifteen minute walk to the coffee shop while the temperature was so low it
nearly seared any exposed skin.

We set aside this time once a week to speak directly to each other's
struggles and sins. We shared rich theological thoughts and exchanged
encouragements. The rest of the week was available to joke around and
shove mashed potatoes into the other's face in the cafeteria. But not this
hour on Friday mornings. That foggy time before the sun was up and the
city was painted in dark blue hues was set aside for intentional deep
conversation.

I really miss those hours.

One of the most fascinating studies I came across in regards to cultures
escaping the deep and the spiritual is Mark Sayers' study of a *superflat*
culture. He writes, "Understanding the Japanese concept of superflat is
key in understanding the context we find ourselves discussing our faith."

It began when the atomic bombs detonated in Japan. 225,000 people died.

In a similar manner to our 9/11 or Columbine, this event shaped the
following years though a sort of collective post traumatic stress disorder.
The Japanese culture responded to the atomic bombs by retreating from
anything of depth to the opposite extreme of all things cute, cuddly, and
superficial. Anything that will distract them from the pain felt in the

depths of their humanity. The Japanese artist Takashi Murakami observed, "Japanese are seeking a spiritual peace and an escape from brutal reality through cute things."

They have become a million miles wide and an inch deep. Sayers continues,

> Murakami has labelled Japanese popular youth culture *superflat* because it lacks any kind of depth. It's visually stimulating but spiritually shallow. Japanese young people are presented with an abundance of consumer choices and technological advancements but they are experiencing what Murakami calls *"empty happiness"*, a sort of cute, cuddly and naïve hell…Japanese young people are craving spiritual depth, answers to the big questions of life, but instead they walk out their door and are confronted with a super cute, super loud, super stimulating, super bright, but ultimately superflat world.

For every reaction, there is an equal and opposite reaction.

In this case, the response of the Japanese people to the slaughter of a quarter-million people was to swing to the opposite end of the spectrum, where the cute animals have giant eyes and long tongues to greet you with a happy lick. There is a fear of intimacy that has developed in Japan, to the degree that people cultivate romantic relationships with computer programs. There are even robotic sensual products available to those who want to be touched while avoiding intimacy with another human being.

Because intimacy requires vulnerability.

For a culture still reeling from collective PTSD, vulnerability is terrifying.

The most interesting part of Sayers' analysis is what happens in Australia's Outback. As an Australian pastor, he has encountered these Japanese pilgrims personally, and what he shares about them is fascinating. Sayers tells the stories of these Japanese youths:

After High School or University they would decide to go on an adventure, they would come to Australia, hire a car and drive out into the utter desolation of the Australian outback desert, where one can drive for days and see nothing. Deprived of stimulation, outside of their superflat world, they would have a spiritual and existential breakdown. By the time they arrived on our church's doorstep, the superflat distraction was detoxed out of their system and the big questions of life, God, human existence and death were now at the forefront of their mind.

I think I need a distraction detox. Although Sayers is writing specifically about Japanese young people, I read these accounts and can't help but see myself in them. I have become someone obsessed with distraction and noise. Our culture may not be as *supercute* as Japan's, but we are well on our way toward being *superflat*.

Our hands twitch if they go too many minutes without touching our phone.

I can't remember the last day I didn't look at a screen.

Sayers comments on western culture, "Our spiritual muscles have atrophied due to lack of use. We are offered a culture that is a million miles wide in terms of opportunities, freedoms and consumer choice, yet that is spiritually an inch deep. Our spiritual voice is being strangled."

Even those of us raised in Christian homes are products of this secular environment. Since the Enlightenment, we have been programmed to think that the visible is all there is. Prior to Nietzsche's "death of God," the Divine played a role in every single part of life. You would prepare for a trip across the country by preparing food, harnessing the horses, and— most importantly—walking through rituals to ward off the evil spirits which would inevitably attack you along the way.

If you didn't do *all* of those things, you were a fool.

But today, we must learn to see through this atheistic culture and look for depth in this *superflat* climate.

We western folks are far from exempt from the touch
Even we Christians may acknowledge God once or twice
day, living largely as if we were dependent only on ourselves. ...
become aware of much of the tones with which I talk about spiritual
things. Especially at Bible college, much of our theological discourse
seems to be more theoretical than tangible. We talk about the Trinity as if
they *may* be one way or another. The incarnation of God is a nice
thought, as is our adoption as children of the Most High, but that's
basically all they are:

Thoughts.

Theories.

Hypotheses.

Our spiritual dialogue concludes with a period as we transition from
thinking about supernatural things to what we're going to put in our
Chipotle burrito.

If God is more of a theory than a person, how can we possibly hope to
have any kind of intimate relationship with Him?

In the wonderful little volume *The Practice of the Presence of God*, Brother
Lawrence calls believers to a constant and unceasing awareness of God's
nearness to us, and to endless conversation with Him:

> We should establish ourselves in a sense of God's Presence by
> continually conversing with Him. It was a shameful thing to quit
> His conversation, to think of trifles and fooleries. In the midst of
> your troubles take solace in Him as often as you can. Lift up your
> heart to Him during your meals and in company...One need not
> cry out very loudly; He is nearer to us than we think."

We Westerners have filled our minds with so much that to set time aside ır God seems trivial, and inviting His presence into every part of our lives seems more like a chore than a comfort. As a result, our relationship with Him is strained and distant.

Is your relationship with God superflat? Is it shiny and cute but only a few inches deep? Take time to step away from the distraction. Find a place that can become your own 'Australian Outback,' where you can escape the noise, screens, and distractions and simply be with God and with yourself. A place where you can ask the deep questions and expect a satisfying response. Deprived of superflat stimulation, we can expect to come face-to-face with the One that dwells in the silence of the desert.

We have become accustomed to a world that does not acknowledge God and His work in it. As science turns over more rocks, it seems there is less space for mystery to exist. This mystery was key for people's understanding of God in the past, as the more mystery there was, the more room there was for God to move. It seems science, philosophy, and technological shifts have eliminated room for God to exist, as our need for Him has essentially evaporated.

But there will always be mystery.

There will always be more rocks to overturn.

And there will always be human souls which long for something more than what our eyes can see and our hands can hold.

Rather than seeing scientific advancements as routes by which to eliminate God, we should see them as paths leading us *to* God, and into deeper intimacy with Him. By better understanding the world, we can better understand the One who made it. Science doesn't eliminate our need for God, but it does change the way we interact with Him. For instance, we can use medicine to heal diseases rather than assume an evil spirit has descended upon our loved ones. We can still stand in awe before a clapping thunderstorm, aware that positive and negative particles are intersecting, instead of fearing the anger of Zeus.

Science and the Enlightenment do not diminish our need for God as much as they lead us to see Him in new ways; we realize more and more the complexity and care with which He made the world, leaving just enough mystery for us to engage with Him on a more-than-physical level.

I was oddly inspired to recognize the presence of God by the 2015 horror film *The VVitch*, which, in addition to being terrifying and beautifully crafted, highlights many Puritanical ways of life in the 1600's. The film focuses on a solitary family of seven who have been exiled from their colony and faces the bleak winter of the New World. The family's baby is snatched by a witch who lives in the woods and appears in several forms throughout the film.

The religious backdrop against which the film is set is what really drew me into the story. Theirs is a life in which every action and motive is weighed against a holy God. As Puritans, they saw nearly every one of their actions (or at least motives) as sinful and they regularly asked for forgiveness. When the baby vanishes (taken by a wolf, they initially believe), the mother fasts, prays and weeps for several days straight, begging for God to have mercy on their family. Over the course of the entire film, the family regularly thanks God for everything He gives them, regardless of how menial and insignificant. Essentially, everything is from God, and every act they committed was done in the presence of God.

They had a constant awareness of Emmanuel; God with them.

I wish I were as constantly aware of God as they are in the film. More often, my religion looks like a few hours on Sunday and maybe a collective few minutes throughout the rest of the week. If I were graded on how much time a week I spend thinking about God and interacting with Him, I would be beyond failing. (Thankfully, that's not how salvation works!)

I think reconstructing a spirituality in which we are more aware of God's constant presence in our lives is a major step in combatting loneliness. One of the last things Jesus told His followers before ascending into heaven is that He will always be with us. Do you ever think about this? In your times of loneliness do you ever recognize the fact that *Jesus is with you?* Whether you have just finished hooking up with a stranger from the bar or are singing in church, Jesus is with you.

I think too many of us have put up a dividing wall in our minds between us and God. We may think, *I'm in church. It's okay to pray here.* But we are scared to approach Him after an especially heinous episode of watching porn or cutting ourselves. We think Jesus didn't really mean it when He promised to be with us *always.* He only meant when we're behaving ourselves and after the priest has prayed for us. That's when He's with us.

No, I think that when Jesus said *always,* He meant *always.*

I like how Bob Goff points out that when Jesus says He will always be with us, He wasn't just saying he would hang out near us and be present close to us. It's more than that. He is with us the way a soldier is *with* another soldier. Or the way a parent is *with* their kid in little league.

God is on our side. He is rooting for us.

He is really *with* us in every sense.

Perhaps some parts of our loneliness come from a failure to realize that God really is constantly with us.

So how do we escape the rhythms of our own culture? It sings the sweet tunes of happiness and materialism. We are programmed daily by advertisements and television shows which teach us what to long for, what to love. It seems that the key to happiness is more, more, more, and then we'll be happy. More friends, less loneliness.

Muyskens wrote, "We live in a culture that esteems accumulation, but the

Christian life is one of subtraction rather than addition."

I daresay our culture is wrong. Modern people are flummoxed by the idea that peace is found by removing things from our lives rather than adding more. We have escaped both the notions that life is most fulfilling when lived in community, and that there is more to this world than what we can see or observe. We are solitary in our construction of our identities, as well as solitary in our spirituality. We confess belief in God with our tongues but live as if He were not always with us. Our culture has framed our lives in a way that distances us from others and from God, and we Christians are still trying to figure out how to react.

I think the key is to learn new dance moves.

A college professor of mine declared from the stage one day, "SAINTS! Everyone loves to dance. God loves to dance! But He wants us to learn the steps."

There are steps in knowing God. There are methods of syncing ourselves with His rhythms more than those of our culture, and they are not always the easy ones. There are steps we can take to reconstruct our communities to look more like unified groups who love each other more than splintered individuals who sometimes get drinks together.

In a culture that encourages shallowness and taking nothing seriously, we can strive to be the ones who rise above the noise and stand for something. We can be the ones who dive beneath shallow connections and a *superflat* spirituality to become people of substance.

People who value relationships and connection.

People who know how to dance.

GOOD WORK/BAD WORK

"I'll be working my hands to the bone,
I'll be working my hands to the bone."
-Besides Daniel, *Learn How To Fight*

I've had 31 jobs in my life and I still can't figure out if that's a good or bad thing to put on my resume. I mean, I'm a fantastic worker, but I can't seem to stay in the same place for too long. I get bored and angsty and move on. Right now, as I juggle personal training, youth ministry, speaking and writing this book, I really feel satisfied with my work life. My jobs are *good work*.

I'll explain.

When I am training clients in the gym, I explain to them the difference between 'good hurt' and 'bad hurt.' 'Good hurt' is when their muscles are burning and they are wearing themselves out in order to grow stronger and more healthy. 'Bad hurt' is when a joint is popping, or there is a spur in a bone somewhere and if they keep doing the movements they will injure themselves. So when a client is doing lunges and cries out in agony, I quickly ask them if it's good or bad hurt (it's usually good and then I call them a weenie).

I think the same is true in our careers. We need to learn the difference between *good work* and *bad work* in order to understand what we do and should be doing with our hands. Good work will push us and grow us and often be difficult, but we come out the other end stronger. Bad work just injures us, stunts growth, and can even be detrimental to those around us.

I've spent a few months working on some kind of philosophy on work, what it is, and how and why we do it. I think my generation often sees work as a means to make money, rather than a fruitful endeavor in itself. Often, our sentiments reflect a culture that is pragmatic in its approach to life, rather than one that works toward the flourishing of all people and of the earth. We often make the mistake of thinking that our work is satisfactory if we have a paycheck at the end of the day, rather than looking at what we have contributed to the world and those around us.

Let's take a look at one extreme of this. Think about a stripper working in a dingy bar on the south side of Chicago. Let's name her Stella.

She makes good money and leaves each night with a hefty wad of cash in her pocket. But her work is not good because it is not fruitful. She does not feed her soul with her work, nor does she contribute to the lives of her customers in a healthy way. Nothing is produced which helps to advance her society or her culture.

Most of all, Stella's work dehumanizes her as a person.

When God gave Adam a job in the Garden of Eden, He did not do it to punish Adam. He didn't do it because Adam had sinned at that point— He gave Adam a job before any sin was committed. God gave man work because God knows that the work of our hands and the things we produce enhance our humanity. Good work gives us fulfillment and satisfaction in ways bad work does not.

Perhaps you feel some sort of loneliness or frustration because the work you do dehumanizes you in some way.

For instance, two of my least favorite jobs were for giant corporations. One was a global retail store and the other was at one of the major fast food chains. I had a five minute window to check in for work, and a five minute window to clock out using my "unique employee number." Everything was scanned in, we had codes to use on the walkie talkies, and everything on the shelves had to be made perfect. All of our orders came from mysterious corporate overseers we never interacted with. I was reprimanded if I spent too much time talking to a customer instead of on my task.

In both jobs, I felt like I was more of a number than a human being.

I wonder if some of our collective loneliness is a result of mass-produced goods and generic merchandise. I mean, compare my experiences in those two massive chains with a local shop where a family and a few employees sell products they are really passionate about.

Think about how much more fulfilled the small shop owners might feel at the end of the day, having sold some things they are passionate and knowledgable about. They build relationships with customers and take their time carefully helping their customers. Compare this to the rushed and frenzied world of gigantic corporations which usher in thousands of customers and pump them through the checkout lines because to them, employees and customers alike are mere means to the end of making more money.

Does your work humanize you or make you feel like a number?

I am writing very abstractly, but think that these examples provide tangible comparisons between good, humanizing work and mass-produced dehumanizing jobs.

Please do not misread me here. Good work can still leave you tired at the end of the day. Just because you're doing a job doesn't mean it won't wear you out and push your boundaries. Often.

I have worked three construction jobs in my life and through them, found that I am not a construction man. Not only does it drain me and become something I dread going to every day, but I'm just not that good at it.

However, I have had bosses and coworkers who *love* working construction. They love the opportunity to work with their hands, sweat, and see the things they have built. The fact that they love the work doesn't mean they never get tired or worn out or exhausted from a long day of moving lumber or framing an office. The fact that we get tired from our job does not mean we are doing bad work. I believe Adam got blisters on his hands before he ever sinned.

God is not against *hard* work, just *bad* work.

I recently sat in on a Theology of Work class at a seminary and the professor listed some attributes of good work. I have already touched on the creative, humanizing and fruitful aspects of good work, but the one that stood out to me the most in this list was Relational.

Good work is relational.

Work does not happen in a vacuum devoid of people, but in the context of society, culture, and other people. There are very few jobs which do not affect other people. Farmers produce crops in order to feed the community, not just themselves. Bankers, plumbers, and salesmen all do work because it aids the lives of other people. There are very few jobs which do not affect others in some way.

I don't write these words in the hopes that no one will benefit from it; teachers don't speak to empty classrooms, nor do plumbers fix toilets no one will ever use. Our work is communal, and helps others when it is done right.

Lonely people often are people trapped in bad jobs. They may be working out of selfish motives, or may simply be part of a dehumanizing company. Good work brings together communities and helps others just as much as it helps the one doing the work.

If you want to figure out how your work touches others, ask yourself specifically how your job affects other people. Waitresses and chefs put food in people's stomachs. Artists stir emotions in their viewers, and mechanics fix cars so people can have reliable transportation. How does your job help other people? Come back to this question whenever you get frustrated with your career and need a reminder of why you do what you do, and why your work is good.

Many of my lonely seasons have been spent either in bad work, or not enough work. When we are bored, we have time for a loneliness and unrest which is rarely felt by people who love what they do and keep themselves busy. These lonely seasons also feel very purposeless or directionless, and I spend excessive time stressing about what my future will look like, or what my *purpose* is.

People without purpose tend to feel very lonely.

I used to lead a Bible study at one of the leading engineering schools in America. The guys and girls who attend this school go on to become millionaires and cure a myriad of diseases and make their own rocket ships for fun. They're brilliant guys, so I was surprised one night when one of them told me he doesn't see the value in the work he is going into. He is going into the world of creating prosthetic limbs and joints for people who are handicapped or injured, yet he didn't see the spiritual merit in his work.

"I won't be teaching people about the Bible and telling them about Jesus like you do," he said to me. I thought he was loopy as a one-legged kangaroo.

Good work doesn't only refer to pastors and theologians. Their work is no more 'holy' than a pilot or a cobra tamer (In fact, many pastors do *bad work* when they work out of pride or a hunger for power or money). I began explaining to my friend that when he does any type of good work, he glorifies God. When he makes high-quality prosthetics for people, he is fulfilling God's call to work just as much as a pastor. His work will be productive, fruitful, creative, and will benefit many people (arguably in a more tangible way than a pastor can).

I hesitate to define good and bad work too rigidly here for a number of reasons. For instance, working construction or trying to make prosthetic limbs would be terrible work for me because I would probably hurt more people than I would help, and I would build crooked houses. But for my friends, it is great work because they are gifted in those areas and love what they do. Two men could have the same CEO job, and one could perform it well and the other very poorly depending on their motives. Greed versus generosity. Each of us is equipped with a certain skill set and collection of passions which can help us find the very best work possible.

However, there will be seasons we are forced to work jobs we don't love, and we should look to these as times to grow. To learn the value of discipline and about becoming a good *worker* even if the *work* we are doing is not ideal. I didn't love working in a local hardware store when I was in middle school, but it taught me about good work ethics and honesty in the business place; about showing up on time and *earning* my money.

When we associate our work with our spiritual lives, it becomes more fulfilling and meaningful. Suddenly we are not just working for a paycheck, but we are working to contribute to our communities and honor God with our hands. For some reason, our Christian culture incorporates things like sex, money, and morals into our spiritual lives, but our work lives have mysteriously been left out of the conversation. As a result, many people in my generation—such as my engineer friend—feel a sort of restlessness, meaninglessness, and lack of direction in their careers, even if they are doing wonderful work.

When this is the case, the New Loneliness tends to arise. We try to fill those areas where we are lacking with sex, drugs, porn, or bad relationships, or maybe we simply distract ourselves with more Netflix or Facebook. Is work something you love putting your hands to, or is it something you endure just to get to the weekend?

Work should satisfy and fulfill us, and when it doesn't, we will quickly go looking for fulfillment in other places.

One of the biggest difficulties in my generation is not necessarily a lack of good work ethics, but a lack of direction. We feel restless because we have so many options we cannot choose one for our career. More than any other time in history, we can see what is out there for us to do, but as any psychologist will tell you, the more options there are, the harder the decision becomes.

High schoolers now know that they could feed orphans in third world countries just as easily as start their own internet company or become a nurse. Nearly every college student I speak with confesses that they have no idea what they're doing with their life, no matter what they are studying at the time. I think the plethora of options presented to us causes more stress and confusion than ever before. To their credit, millennials have reported that they would rather make less money for a more meaningful job that suits them well. However, when it comes time to pick a direction for our career we are just as lost.

I think this mindset has more to do with fear than indecision.

A mentor of mine once asked me, "If you could do anything in the world and didn't have to worry about time or money, and you couldn't fail, what would you do?"

My response was probably similar to everyone else who has been asked that question: "Oh, I don't know. I don't think it's very realistic. I don't know if the right doors will open. I don't know if the money will show up....."

Over time I realized that rather than working toward what I really wanted to do, I was just wasting time and working to make money. Teaching rock climbing and delivering pizza are not bad jobs, but they were crutches to me at the time because they allowed me to pay my bills without pushing me toward what I'm really gifted in and what I should have been working toward. I was scared that things wouldn't come through, or the money would run out while I was working toward what I wanted to do, or I would embarrass myself, or, or, or....

We are really good at making up excuses.

Are there things you are putting off out of fear or uncertainty?

Now, this is not the book (and I am not the author) to give you one blanket solution for finding your purpose or direction in your life. My hope in this chapter is to help us walk through the ways that the absence of work or purpose in many of our lives *has* led to a sort of loneliness and angst.

One day in the summer of 2013, I was walking down the aisle in Wal-Mart and thinking about my own purpose in my life. I tried to zoom out as far as I could in order to see myself in the context of a larger picture and try from there to delineate what my role was.

My conclusion was a simple one which I am still trying to incarnate. I realized that my purpose—and in some ways, the purpose of every Christian—is to make disciples; to lead people to Jesus in whatever way possible. I realized that this is the only thing I can spend my life doing that will last beyond my lifetime.

However, as I said, delving into the specifics of this simple purpose is much easier said than done. *How* do I make disciples and what methods do I use? Do I do this as a youth pastor, missionary, writer, speaker, or all of the above? Those are all activities, but knowing the purpose—the why

—behind them is what really matters. I think figuring out your purpose in the first step, and putting skin on it is the next step. What do you want your life to look like, and what steps will you take to get there?

I tell you that story to point out that it was 3 years ago and I am only a little closer to finding out what I'll be doing with "the rest of my life." The truth is, life is going on right now whether you're aware of it or not, whether you planned for it or not. You can waste time wondering what you'll be doing with "the rest of your life," or you can start working now.

Test things out.

Find out what you're good at by trying as many things as possible. That's one of the great parts about our option-riddled culture is that we *do* have these opportunities to be specialized in certain areas. I have found out plenty of things I am *not* good at only because I've tried them out for a year or two and now can confidently say, "I've tried it and it's not for me."

The busier you are, the less time you'll have to think about how lonely you are. Not only that, but you'll be actively meeting and interacting with people along the way.

The American maxim teaches us that *if we love what we do, we will never work a day in our lives*. I don't think this is true. If we love what we do, then we will love our job and do good work. I think we are called to work. We are called to *good* work, because good work glorifies God. Good work satisfies and fulfills us. The absence of work leads to unhealthy habits and lifestyles. When work is just a way to stack up money, we can easily become greedy if we don't maintain the value of the work itself.

Often our misunderstandings of work and the absence of purpose can lead to disappointment and frustration in our lives which can look an awful lot like New Loneliness. If you have no direction or momentum in your life, there is a good chance this is contributing to your feelings of loneliness. As I said above, productive work is relational. It touches other people and builds community. Therefore it makes sense that a lack of work (or a lack of *good* work) would contribute to isolation and irritation.

This is amplified when we feel purposeless or are having trouble seeing ourselves in the context of a much larger picture. Our culture puts so much emphasis on the individual and the feeding of the individual's ego and life that when we feel like there is no purpose to our lives, incredible amounts of stress and fear set in.

I think we can battle this in a number of ways. The first is to relieve the stress of needing to have a purpose or a career path *right now*. It is alright to have what I call a 'gradient period.' a fade or a transition time to adjust from one season to the next. Instead of racing from college to a career of 40 years, we can take our time, experiment, and find out what we really love through trial and error.

The next step is to honestly ask yourself (as I do regularly...and I'm not always happy with the answer) "Am I a lazy person?" Laziness is something we often excuse because it's not quite as blatant a sin as, say, adultery. But laziness contributes to loneliness, purposelessness, isolation, and unfruitfulness just as much as any other sin. If you find yourself engaging in patterns of laziness, try pushing yourself a little bit. Find more meaningful work and produce 'good fruit,' whatever that looks like in your life.

Perhaps your problem is not a lack of work, but simply a lack of *good work,* or at least, work that is not best suited to you. Maybe a change is necessary and you can try something else for a while. If work is damaging to your soul or your personhood, it is most likely bad work. You don't need to be a hitman or a prostitute to be doing bad work, but if your work dehumanizes you then it is not a good thing.

In light of all of this, find good work to do and be productive.

Be fruitful.

Work often and work well, even if your job is not glamorous or enjoyable.

A Millennial Hymn

I have learned that the best thrift stores
cannot be Google, Bing or Yelped;
They're spread by word of mouth
without requesting Siri's help.
I have learned a plastic zip tie
holds my hood shut while I drive
across the states in my Corolla
just to feel some more alive.
I've learned that cops don't let you trespass
just "to get a better picture,"
and that nine times out of ten,
I'll feel remorse after I've kissed her.

Because I've learned that people come and go—
or maybe I'm the one who's leaving,
always packing up a bag because it's better over there
...so I'm believing.

I've worked a half a thousand jobs
and I've made almost that much money,
and I'll make light of just how broke I am
even though it isn't funny.

I can't name every president,
but I'm fluent in memeology,
and I'd probably be richer
if I'd not studied theology.
Yet here I sit, broke af
and borderline content.
I'm loving what I'm doing
though it won't make me a cent.

BIG PLEASURE

If any thing is sacred, the human body is sacred.
-Walt Whitman

Last year I made the mistake of telling the writer at TMZ that I'm still a virgin. He broadcast that fact across the internet, it was nabbed by countless other news sources, and to this day, people will come up and ask me about it. They never want to know about my travels, my writing, my friends, my family, or any other aspect of my life.

Just my sex life.

(Which still doesn't exist.)

Our culture is obsessed with sex.

Most people cannot comprehend the concept of a 25-year-old virgin, yet here I am, extant and tangible.

And sometimes lonely.

It makes sense that most of us would try to plug up the dam of our own loneliness with the satisfying waters of sex and pornography. After all, how much closer can two people get than when they are making love? It is designed to be the most intimate action between two people, yet our culture has taken these intimate moments between a husband and wife and splattered them across billboards, television screens, and nearly every page of the internet. Not only in pornography either. Mostly-naked women adorn countless advertisements and banners in every corner of America.

To make matters worse, our culture belittles our own sexual brokenness.

My roommate in college once pointed out that we joke the most about the things we are most broken over. I was about to respond to him with a witty joke until I realized he was right. In fact, he could not have been more right.

Those who were sexually abused in their youth are often the ones making the most crude sexual jokes and belittling the importance of sex. Because for them, it has been ruined and rather than address their brokenness and try to heal from it, they point fingers at it and make jokes.

Joking distances us from our pain.

The problem with joking about our brokenness extends far beyond our personal conversations. Turn on nearly any sitcom and you'll quickly realize what the vast majority of the jokes are about: Sex.

Every punchline is about sex.

Every innuendo is a reference to another dirty act.

Many of the plots even revolve around one promiscuous encounter or another; who left their underwear where at who's apartment?

Our society is beyond broken in our sexuality, and the most we have to offer is a witty one-liner about it. After my roommate pointed out to me that we joke most about what we are most broken over, I realized that many of my jokes revolved around pornography and masturbation. He was right.

My own humor revealed the very things I was trying to belittle and distance myself from. In an attempt to minimize the impact of my own sin and pain, I would make jokes in an attempt to convince myself they weren't really all that bad.

I think many of us turn to sex and pornography out of a hope that it will cure the void of loneliness within us. I have found, however, that this is a gross misunderstanding of sex and the context for which it was created.

Whenever we seek out porn online or head to a club to hook up, we are trying to invite someone into the most vulnerable and intimate parts of who we are. We want the nearness of their physical body to reflect an emotional nearness which is simply not there.

When a husband and a wife are married and make love on their honeymoon, they do not do so as strangers; they do so as lovers. Years before, there was some sort of initial attraction. Then dates. Then movies and conversations and stories together. They become emotionally attached and grow together spiritually. Their bank accounts eventually overlap and become one, so there is even financial unity.

Then when they come together on their wedding night, the physical intimacy mirrors the time they have poured into their emotional, spiritual, financial and sacrificial intimacy.

A few years ago I was in a coffee shop with a friend who had recently been married. He and his wife were virgins when they were married, and he began telling me about their wedding night.

"It wasn't really grand or surprising," he remembered. "It just felt like the next logical progression in our relationship. There weren't fireworks or anything, it was just me and her loving each other."

He said it with such candor and comfort that the scene he painted was beautiful. It seemed like his wedding night was not one full of insecurities or awkwardness, but a progression of love for two people who had put time into building a healthy relationship.

Many of us are hungry for that level of intimacy, but are impatient. We want to jump straight to the union and the gratification, so we hook up or look at porn in an attempt to fill the void within.

The thing is, sex doesn't heal our loneliness; intimacy does.

Saint Augustine graphically recounts his own awakening to his lustful desires: "From the mud of my fleshly desires and my erupting puberty belched out murky clouds that obscured and darkened my heart until I could not distinguish the calm light of love from the fog of lust." He identified his craving for sex as an artificial substitute for true love and authentic connection.

Casual sex is simply an attempt to fill this void with *something* that puts another human body near our own. Surely sexual intimacy will satiate our need for holistic intimacy, right?

The problem with the purity movement of the past several decades is that they framed their philosophy in a negative way:

"DON'T have sex until you're married." I feel like so much caution and guilt was squeezed into that generation that rebellion was inevitable.

What would happen if we reframed the way we look at sex and chastity? What if we saw our chastity as a positive thing? We could not be simply inhibiting our sexual urges, but making them even greater. What if we traded in cheap sex for something truly great and beautiful? Amber Lapp writes for Comment Magazine,

> In this vision, the choice to delay sex is not seen as a repression of a natural desire, but as a way to discipline a desire in order to strengthen it and enjoy an even greater good, just as we discipline our desires for certain foods in order to enjoy good health and long life.

She continues in the article to argue that the true sexual revolutionaries today are those who chase after a greater conception of love: Those who actually battle their urges in order to cultivate a greater future intimacy with their spouse. It's easy to give in and sleep around, but the true difficulty is patience and resisting the desire for quick and easy hook ups.

One day a friend and I were having a conversation via text. He told me about why sex is so great, about how spiritual and meaningful it is to him, and that's why I should be participating as well. Apparently I was missing out because there was this spectacular and intimate entity that was so rich and fulfilling to him.

In the very next text, he said that's why he has slept with about 150 people. And continues to.

It caught me off guard because of how beautifully he described the magic of sex, only to follow it up with such a gratuitous number of people with whom he had shared this 'intimacy.' Is it really intimate if it is shared with hundreds of people? Somehow though, this fits within our culture's framework of sex: If it feels good, do it...

...just don't think about it too much.

Tucker Max became famous for writing about his myriad sexual escapades and crazy nights of partying. For over a decade he was the poster boy for Bro-Culture, which insisted that sleeping around and escaping sobriety was the way to a fun, fulfilling life. Max created a new genre: "Fratire." He was the first author to simultaneously have three non-fiction books on the New York Times best seller list.

But then he got bored.

"As crazy as my single life was," he wrote on his blog, "my 'marriage' life is boring (at least, to other people). Veronica is an amazing person, we've been together for almost two years now, and our relationship is incredibly fulfilling and rewarding to both of us." Max confessed that in marriage and commitment, he found something "incredibly fulfilling." He added, "There's not much else to say. That's the thing about happy, loving relationships; they are great to be in, but they don't make for great stories."

But he may be wrong here.

In her article, Amber Lapp noted that many people in our generation look nostalgically at our grandparents' relationships, and how amazing it is that these people can live life together for 40, 50, 60 years, and we are depressed to realize that that tradition of commitment has all but crumbled.

The film *Up* comes to mind, which opens with a silent narrative about a young boy and girl in the early 1900's who fall in love. We watch as they both long for adventure, mature together, and eventually marry. They live life together, grow older, find out she cannot have children, and then she falls down.

The amazing thing about this five minute vignette is that not a word is spoken, yet we are drawn into the soft and constant love between these two. We watch as she can't make it up their favorite picnic hill and winds up in a hospital bed. In the next scene we see him at her funeral, an old man now leaning on his cane.

Even writing this synopsis out in this coffee shop, I'm getting a lump in my throat recalling it. The animators at Pixar did a phenomenal job telling this short visual story.

Whenever anyone brings up *Up*, the first thing they mention is the first five minutes. It sticks to our brain like honey because the creative team truly tapped into something deep within us: Our desire for intimacy and commitment. Not a fleeting sort of physical encounter, but a deep and rich intertwining of our lives. The explosive mixture of two souls. A shared passion for adventure or piano; an appreciation for Fauvist painters or coffee roasting.

These stories stick with us because, counter to our current cultural narrative, they speak of something truly difficult: Lifelong commitment; a singular vision for one person, rather than the rainbow spectrum of cramming as many people into our bed as possible.

Perhaps this is why our sexual mores have left us wanting: Our escape into pornography or our weekly hook-ups cannot stand up to the levels of mutual trust and commitment offered in chaste relationships and marriage.

Logically, this makes sense.

If you can trust your virgin boyfriend to abstain from sleeping around when he is single, you won't have to worry about him cheating on you in marriage. If he was able to keep it in his pants for all the time he was single, why would you have to worry about him cheating now that he has an outlet for his sexual urges?

Not only will the fear and distrust be gone, but the heights of joy will be elevated. I know a man who simply cannot shut up about his wife and how great she is. It's as if she is constantly on his mind and all other women are invisible. The two were married as virgins, so his experience of sexual intercourse with her is ridiculously rich and satisfying.

"It's like she's almost a god to him," one co-worker noted.

I think the risk we face in encouraging sexual chastity is being seen as prudes. Anyone who knows me personally knows the opposite to be true of me. I could not be *more* excited to give my virginity to my wife, and my (aggravating) patience in the matter has only heightened my anticipation for the future delight I'll have in my wife. It is my *high* view of sex and eager expectation for pleasure that has caused me to cling to my virginity, rather than what our culture calls a 'suppression of my natural urges.'

I want bigger pleasure, not smaller pleasure.

Big pleasure comes from two people living life together and knowing each other intimately. Sex gets better with age, according to every married couple I've asked, as you get to know the other's body intimately, just as you have gotten to know their personality and their soul.

"It's just good to be naked with the same person," my dad once told me.

Small pleasure comes from countless sexual escapades, each one leaving us only more hungry and unsatisfied because we are not really *known*. It's like trying to get full by eating Kit-Kats. It may be a quick and enjoyable snack, but when it's over, you are left hungry, unlike the experience of eating a home-cooked four-course meal with love, time and effort poured into its preparation.

Please don't misread me though. I think one of the worst offshoots of the purity movement was the enormous amount of shame it caused. These Christian teenagers who lost their virginity after pledging to purity would be consumed with so much shame that they either rebelled against Christianity altogether, or sought to justify themselves with a series of hermeneutical gymnastics which would make your pastor's head spin.

The goal is not to shame people who have slept around, but to encourage them to a life of richer pleasure. A life of deep and rich intimacy with a spouse, rather than a lonely one spent scouring clubs and bars for a few scraps of satisfaction. This is an invitation to rich pleasure and deep intimacy, not a shameful condemnation.

My pornography addiction started when we were walking home from the bus stop one day. The boy who lived across the street from me, affectionately named Big Jake, was telling me about this 'normal thing all guys do.'

"Every guy does it when he feels like it," Jake explained. "Even my dad does it when he's in the mood."

We were in seventh grade and I doubt Big Jake had any idea what huge bearing that small conversation would have on the rest of my life. In fact, I recently passed the point where that day was over twelve years ago—meaning I've been wrestling against the ineffably destructive beast of pornography for over half the time I've been alive.

It's hard to overstate the negative effects of pornography in our lives. Whether we speak of marriage, families, relationships, friendships, self-esteem, or careers, porn has a way of sticking its fingers deep into every deep dark crevasse of our lives. I had no idea that what Big Jake introduced me to that fall afternoon would have such resounding effects throughout the course of my life.

Porn takes the detrimental outcomes of a one night stand and combines them with the secrecy and ease of checking a text message. It's everywhere. It lives in my pocket and yours. When you hook up with someone after a party, you sleep with one person. In one pornography session, you can be exposed to dozens of different bodies in mere minutes.

The essence of pornography is novelty.

Once you have exhausted one person's body, click on to the next one. You get tired of hers? Move on.

Of course this is not so with long-term committed relationships. When you marry someone, you not only marry their soul, personality, and spirit; you marry their body as well. And you commit to it and vow to be faithful to their *body*.

The nature of pornography is such that it rewires our minds to crave new things constantly. There is no such thing as a static porn addiction. What I mean by that is, you will never be satisfied with what you are watching on the screen. We will always crave more graphic and twisted things the longer we are entangled in its claws. Falling into the trap of pornography is like stepping on a sled at the top of a hill. You cannot stay at the same place, but must always fly downward, deeper and deeper into its grasp and into more depraved imagery.

As Christians, we should be terrified of pornography. The thought of looking at it should scare us. The older I get, the more stories I have heard about porn creeping its way into a marriage and destroying it from the inside. One of my biggest fears is divorce, especially due to my own sins of pornography and lust. My future wife deserves so much more than that.

Pope John Paul II observed that "the problem with pornography is not that it shows *too much* of the person, but that it shows *far too little*." In other words, people are much more than bodies. We have thoughts and feelings and personalities, and all of these mix together to create who we are. Our bodies are a part of that equation of course, but pornography takes entire humans and reduces them to nothing more than bodies to be used for our own consumption and pleasure.

One thing I have noticed about pornography is that it is the logical extreme of a consumeristic and entertained culture. By watching Netflix, and even by logging into Facebook and seeing the little red numbers, we feed our brains a steady stream of chemicals to keep them satiated. The problem again is, our brains are not static. They change and always want more of these chemicals. We want higher numbers of likes to feed our brains those chemicals.

Pornography is the extreme of feeding our brains the chemicals they crave. They cause a spike in our dopamine—the chemical that gives a feeling of satisfaction and pleasure—which our brains then get accustomed to. But since our brains are not static organs, they begin to want more and more dopamine, leading us into darker and darker corners of the internet in order to satisfy our brain's hunger.

For many of us porn begins as an innocent curiosity or a longing to alleviate the nagging pain of being alone, but it quickly evolves into a full-blown addiction on the same level of heroine and cocaine addicts. And its use is employed in much the same way. Our pain is numbed and reality is escaped, if only for a few minutes.

Porn takes away the loneliness much faster than a movie or Netflix—mainly because of the dopamine releases it triggers—but the shame which ensues after each episode is intense. Because of porn, many men and women in the church today don't see themselves as worthy of marriage or love. Pornography creates a 'shame cycle,' in which someone feels lonely and acts out sexually somehow. Afterward, the feelings of dirtiness and shame rush in and convince the person they are *bad*. After a while, whether it's a few hours or a few weeks, the shame has set in and the person is completely convinced again that they are a bad person, unworthy of love. Eventually, this sends them on another hunt for artificial love online, and the cycle repeats itself.

When we get caught in these traps of pornography-fueled shame cycles, we need to remember that shame is not where we live. We are not called to be a shameful people, but a beloved people.

The difference between guilt and shame is, guilt is the knowledge that I have *done* something bad, but shame is the feeling that *I am* bad.

Healthy guilt should call us to repent and change our actions, but more often, we fill ourselves up with shame instead which leads us back into these sexual addictions.

Pornography has become the plague of our generation for a number of reasons. It is accessible as the nearest screen, which is typically in our pocket. It feels good and seems to satisfy a deep longing within us. John Eldredge wrote, "What makes pornography so addictive is that more than anything else in a man's life, it makes him feel like a man without ever requiring a thing of him." The same is true of women of course. Porn offers a chance to feel loved and appreciated without causing us to risk exposure or insecurities the way real relationships do.

Porn is a cause, fuel, and escape from loneliness. We turn to it when we feel lonely, but the shame it causes results in more isolation. It's an endless cycle that only grace, love, and relationship with God can heal. The best book I have ever read on sexual addiction is *Surfing for God* by my friend Michael Cusick. If you or someone you love struggles with this, please read it for a much more in-depth examination of today's pornography problem.

We are not called to walk in bondage and addiction, but in freedom. Bondage to pornography or one-night-stands is not freedom, but quite the opposite. They cause shame which act as catalysts to our loneliness. Find freedom and healing by spending time with God, realizing your belovedness and delighting in rich relationship with a God who is near.

Good to be Naked

He sat me down and said
it's not as much about what she looks like on the outside,
my grandfather told me,
although that is nice,
it's not as much about her suntanned body
as it is
the sunshine that shoots from her eyes
even when she's sixty-six,

he said,
sure sex is great
and a good body is exciting at first,
but eventually,
it's just good to be naked,
it's nice to be naked with the same old person,
my grandpa said,

and some people
think their parents are still chaste
and never *do it,*
but I'm glad my grandparents
are still magnets growing old,
as I hope to be old with someone
too.

WHY I WAS THE WORST LIFEGUARD EVER

"Jesus knew the pain you feel,
He can save and He can heal,
Take your burden to the Lord
and leave it there."
-Washington Phillips, *Take Your Burden to the Lord*

When I was at my second college, I worked as a lifeguard at one of the local rec centers. Being a lifeguard combines the boringness of watching weeds grow with the having-to-hear-kids-screaming-all-day-ness of nannying, so needless to say, it was not a dream job.

The lifeguard stand was right next to the diving boards so I had a front row view of the amateur acrobats that would dive and flip from the one and the three meter boards. When the pool was full, this was the height of entertainment. Watching skilled—or even not so skilled divers—perform was like theater to my brain on the verge of ennui.

One day, I came up with an even better strategy to combat the tedium. I started carrying spare change in my fanny pack and chatting with the 5th graders who were jumping off the boards.

"I'll give you a quarter if you belly flop off the low dive," I murmured to one of the braver looking boys. "Fifty cents if you do it off the high dive."

His eyes lit up.

I could see his brain calculating how many bellyflops could buy a popsicle from the vending machine.

He did that rapid duck waddle you do at swimming pools when you're in a hurry but don't want to get scolded by the lifeguard for running, and climbed the ladder to the one meter board. I wasn't too concerned about him getting hurt, since he was a bigger boy with a little bit more... protection around his midsection than some of the other kids. A little more belly to flop.

He ran to the tip of the board, spread his arms, and lay into a beautiful bellyflop upon the water. He rose to the surface with a big goofy grin on his face and swam over to the foot of my stand. Once he had hoisted his pink belly up onto the deck, he held up his palm with eager expectation.

Right away, the other boys saw what had happened and flocked the stand where I sat, their benevolent king. They talked over one another, eager to earn their silver coin, vying for my attention to let them go up and prove their merit. I laughed and shushed them. I announced that I want one brave volunteer to ascend the high dive and bellyflop from three meters up.

Eventually one boy was selected and slowly climbed the ladder. He was not as plump as the first boy, but this thought didn't cross my mind until afterward. Not only was he not plump, he was skinny, like a lowercase L with arms. The kind of kid who shivers when it's sunny and 75.

Seconds later, the scrawny kid had summited the three meter board and was slowly trembling his way to the edge. He looked down at us, stories below him, and I probably held up a few quarters or something as a reminder of what he was flopping for.

He toed the edge of the plank and was suddenly airborne, free falling toward the water.

He made contact and caused a minimal amount of disturbance to the water like a twig hitting a pond.

Then he just stayed there for a few seconds.

He was too light to sink very deep below the surface, so he just kind of floated,

facedown,

and spread eagle.

I rose to my feet.

His body reanimated and he feebly doggy paddled to the side. He grabbed the edge, pulled his face up to the drain that ran along the side, and puked into it. It wasn't much puke—just a little puke from a little guy.

I felt awful so I overpaid him. I think I gave him 75 cents.

And that's my chapter on the Theology of Loneliness! Hope you enjoyed!

But really, why the h-e-c-k did I begin the theology chapter with the story of me paying kids to bellyflop off the high dive?

I think too often, we see Jesus as no more than a lifeguard. He is there, hanging out beside our pool, but not really engaging with us very much.

He is there if we really get in trouble, but he's not very good at engaging our every day life.

He stays dry while we're wet.

There may have been one time, two thousand years ago, he hopped in the pool and felt our wetness, but for the most part, he is pretty distant. Maybe we don't picture Jesus laughing at our pain like I did with the boys, but at least he's there if we ever *really* need him. And he'll give us a few quarters when the pain subsides.

We see him as an external observer, unable to partake in our pain. We're the scrawny little boy, struggling to get by, living in the pain of the present moment, and the lifeguard is just idly sitting nearby. Of course the metaphor breaks down pretty quickly, but there is an idea I want to focus on:

We often think Jesus is far away from us, from our suffering and from our loneliness.

I can't help but think that the image of 'pure, gentle, harmless, kind Jesus' came from our watered-down American Christian upbringing. We can't possibly imagine Jesus suffering—except for those hours on the cross— because He is kind and nice and sweet. Much of our Christianity knows little of *cruciformity*, or becoming like Christ in His sufferings. We have traded that version of Jesus for one who gives us happy lives and a slew of marriage and self-help books.

But the crucified Jesus knows nothing of self-help.

He makes no promises of earthly riches or comfort.

Even before He was conceived, the prophet Isaiah foretold that Jesus would be a Man of Sorrows, acquainted with deepest grief (Isaiah 53:3). Not only was He rejected by his friends and family as He hung on the cross, but He cried out that He felt abandoned by the God of the universe, by His Father with whom He had known eternal relationship.

This is a profound theological quandary, but I doubt any human can, in this life, feel the depth of rejection Jesus felt as He hung on that tree.

The more theologically-minded of you may wonder how a member of the Trinity—eternally in relationship with the other two—can comprehend what it is to be alone. Jesus mentions in John 17 that prior to the creation of the world, the three of them were alive and loving one another in perfect relationship. So how could God possibly know what it feels like to have these deep feelings of loneliness? How could Jesus accuse the Father of forsaking Him as he dangled, bloody and withering on the cross?

Not only did Jesus experience abandonment by His Father, but the Father had to walk through the grief of losing a child. He resonates with the pain of parents who have lost children in childbirth or car accidents. He lost the Son with whom He had spent eternity past, knowing nothing but unbroken, perfect relationship.

I think it's easy to read the account of Jesus' suffering and wonder what those couple days thousands of years ago mean to us today. *Jesus is back in heaven now, right? He's not suffering anymore, so he probably forgot what it's like, right?*

I often find myself asking the same thing before realizing who it is I'm dealing with. I'm not dealing with a man who can easily forget the past. Nor am I dealing with a man who escapes his emotions and seeks to dull the agony. In the words of my pastor Andrew, "Don't you know??" he thunders from the pulpit, "It is *God* with whom we deal!"

When we talk about God, we speak of One who created emotions and therefore knows them to the deepest degree. He has experienced them on far deeper levels than any human can.

He has been angrier than we will ever be.

He has been more broken hearted than we'd ever want to be.

He experiences more joy than we've ever hoped to experience.

He has been lonelier than we would dare imagine.

We speak of God who could never forget the pain of losing His Son, or the agony of being separated from His Father. He remembers all things and holds them near His chest for all eternity.

We speak of Jesus, the God-man who refused the wine-soaked sponge which would have eased His suffering on the cross (Mark 15:23). The Roman soldiers would offer their victims this cocktail of wine mixed with gall as a way to anesthetize and reduce their suffering. But Jesus turned it down because He did not want to escape the pain He was experiencing, despite how horrific it was.

His pain was so intense in fact, the Romans had to invent a new word to describe it. They realized that the pain of being crucified was so beyond comprehension that a new term emerged:

Excruciating.

Ex is the Greek prefix 'out of,' and *crux*, 'a cross.' The pain was so severe it could only come out of a cross, yet Jesus turned down the opportunity to reduce His pain by rejecting the anesthetic wine.

Jesus lived a life devoid of shortcuts or coping mechanisms.

Look at His first reaction when He hears of John the Baptist's death. He retreats by Himself in a boat to be alone. He didn't pick up a copy of *The New Yorker* and whisk away the pain with some humor columns.

Again, watch what Jesus does when He learns of His friend Lazarus' death (John 11:35). We often toss this verse around as a bit of trivia without giving much thought to its implications.

"Jesus wept."

God wept.

God...

cries.

Jesus knew He was about to call out Lazarus' name and raise him from the dead, but He still takes time to weep. He mourns the death of His friend. To Him, there is no circumventing reality. As much as we try to avoid looking at our own situation, Jesus did not. He would not try to cure His loneliness by scouring Facebook, taking a few tequila shots, or watching Friends reruns until He laughed away His troubles.

I think that as Christians, we are also called to this level of sympathy. We must recognize that when seasons of darkness surround us like a fog, we have opportunities to grow in our sympathy toward others. So when others walk through similar valleys, we can partake in their sadness rather than merely be bystanders witnessing the event.

One woman who embodied this was Mother Teresa. One of her close friends, Brian Kolodiejchuk said, "She understood very well when people would share their horror stories, their pain and suffering of being unloved, lonely. She would be able to share that empathy because she herself was experiencing it."

Mother Teresa had one of the longest recorded "Dark Nights of the Soul" on record, lasting roughly 50 years and not lifting until shortly before her death. The Dark Night of the Soul was a term coined in a poem by a Spanish monk named John of the Cross which described a removal of the tangible presence of God for the purpose of purifying the soul of the believer. These Dark Nights are often described as torturous, as if God had utterly rejected the believer. He even removes the joy of His presence so the believer learns to love God more purely, rather than for pleasure. John of the Cross described them as agonizing to the point of removing all desires for earthly pleasures, so when the Christian comes out the other side, they are more free from the longings for this world and bound ever closer to Christ.

He was an intense dude.

Mother Teresa did not let her record-setting Dark Night of the Soul keep her from being faithful to God, or loving others. She saw it as an opportunity to empathize with others and incarnate the same levels of despair and loneliness they found themselves in.

Don't waste your own Dark Nights.

Don't waste your loneliness.

Be present in it and see it as a means to love others in a more deep, more rich way. In doing so, we become more like Christ, who also came to earth in order to know us and our suffering. We are invited to know Him in His suffering (Philippians 3:10), as this will draw us closer to Him and to others around us.

In the earlier chapter on the pain of loneliness, I talked about the hopelessness of Jesus hanging on the cross. He was rejected by both God and man. He was alone on the hill, abandoned and publicly shamed. If that's the fate of the Son of God, then what chance do we possibly have in combatting loneliness? How can we possibly expect a better outcome?

Whenever we look at Jesus, the scorned God-man, hanging on the cross on Friday afternoon, we must remember that the story does not end there. Jesus is not still on that tree to this day.

We may get hung up on Friday, but we must never forget that Sunday's coming.

When we speak about Jesus, the God of the Bible, we must always conclude with hope. We may be atop Golgotha on Friday, but we can never forget Sunday is coming. There is no possible outcome in which evil prevails or loneliness overcomes. Jesus absorbed all of our suffering and left it on the cross. He took our loneliness and rejection; our shame and our sins, and put them all to death.

We often think of Jesus' work on the cross as performing some kind of transaction: We give Him our sins and He gives us eternal life. *Cha-ching.* While this is true to some degree, I would argue that it's not deep enough. It doesn't affect my broken mind or your perpetual depression. Jesus' crucifixion only really matters if He actively participates *with* us in the things we go through. This is why the incarnation—God becoming man, wrapping Himself in our own skin and tendons—is so important.

Unless Jesus descended and became one with our humanity, we have no hope of ascending and becoming one with Him.

If we look at the lifeguard analogy through that lens, the story would have a much different outcome. The scrawny boy (us) would stand atop the high dive, shivering as per usual, but I (Jesus) would climb up after him. I would have told him to climb back down and sit in my lifeguard seat, so he could watch as I bellyflop.

Then I would walk to the end of the board and toss my arms up, falling into the most beautiful bellyflop he'd ever seen. I would lay motionless in the water, leaving the crowd of boys to wonder what had become of their once strong lifeguard and savior. But moments later, I would come back to life, swim to the side, and puke into the drain. I would take on the full experience of the pain felt by the scrawny little boy.

I wouldn't just watch and sympathize.

I wouldn't just cringe and hand him his three quarters.

I would shove him out of the way and take the full experience of his pain from him.

Because this is what Jesus does for us: He does not simply sit on the side and sympathize with our pain or loneliness. He doesn't just let us suffer by ourselves and then reward us at the end. He takes on the full embodiment of our pain, and pain we will never experience, by coming to earth as a man. He took no shortcuts when He experienced life here on earth, but embraced every ounce of His life, including the painful parts,

the lonely parts,

the tearful parts,

the parts where your heart breaks.

the parts where your friend dies,

the parts where your parents reject you,

et al.

11/28/2014

I'm aching in a place I can't name,
it's an old familiar sort of pain
but I'm living in this place that's all right
when I drive out into the night.
You're clutching some pieces of me
like a fifty-one majority.
And I'm feeling with a new patch of skin
that's not desensitized to my sin,
but I'm hoping that You love with eyes closed;
the heavenly gaze is what I fear most.
But I'm finding that You love Your grace;
like a penny heads-down I'm flat on my face
because this work You began isn't done yet.
There's this song that won't let me forget
and it's all written down in my chest,
cause I've tried it all out and collapsed in Your rest.

SILENCE

"Be still and know that I am God."
-Psalm 46:10

I heard a story once about a woman who went to her therapist and asked him to tell her what was wrong with her.

"I think you're depressed," he said after a few minutes of listening to her story.

"I can't be depressed!" she replied. "I'm always going out with friends and partying and dancing!"

"Well that's exactly what I would do if I were depressed," the therapist answered.

It's not until we can sit quietly with ourselves and be at peace that we will really feel less lonely. Too often, we think the solution to our loneliness is adding more people, but perhaps the problem has more to do with our interior than our surroundings. Sure, it's easier to dress the wound with money, some friends, new clothes, and a raging club downtown, but what good is that doing for your soul? (Don't get me wrong: I love dancing. Just not as an escape from problems.)

Blaise Pascal famously wrote that the most difficult thing a human being can ever do is sit quietly in a room alone for an hour. Why are we so terrified of being alone? Even sitting alone and doing absolutely nothing is work in itself. We have to force ourselves to do it!

I saw this exemplified recently at my birthday dinner with Swaggy Pete. Swaggy Pete is one of my greatest friends. He is the chillest, coolest, Matthew McConaughey-est man you'll ever meet, a philosopher disguised in the hip garb of a transient bohemian. Whenever I sit across from Swaggy Pete, I always learn something. As a human being, he reminds me to slow down.

As the two of us were enjoying our gourmet North Side of Chicago tater tots, amply doused in truffle aioli cream and garlic sprinkling, a married couple sat down at the table directly next to ours. Pete and I had been talking about some of the struggles we had been having this summer with various things. It was a much needed confession of our sins. The night was perfect for it too. We were seated on the outdoor patio as the sky pinked into a warm dusk.

As we were chatting, the husband's cell phone went off. Swaggy Pete and I did nothing, of course, because people's cell phones ring in public all the time. But then it kept ringing—one of those redundant electronic songs which is fun if you're in a club, letting the bass take over for your heart in pumping blood through your body, but when punching through tinny cell phone speakers is just annoying noise.

Then I realized his phone was not ringing.

154

He had played the song on his phone.

Not so odd, I thought. *He probably just wanted to show her a song.*

He didn't.

This man set his phone on the table and let the small staticky sounds fill the restaurant. Song after song, he talked to his wife over the thin beats emanating from his phone. Their table was less than two feet from ours, so Swaggy Pete and I heard every single song on his techno playlist over the course of our formerly pleasant dinner together.

Neither Pete or I said anything of course—he is too chill and I was too into the tater tots to risk spoiling them with fisticuffs—but we discussed it after the fact. We never talked to the man, but I can speculate what made him spoil an otherwise beautiful dinner with the woman he loves. I think it has to do with a cultural reality much larger than one couple.

We as a society are terrified of silence.

We are addicted to noise and distraction.

Even in the 1940's, pastor Dietrich Bonhoeffer wrote, "We are so afraid of silence that we chase ourselves from one event to the next in order not to have to spend a moment alone with ourselves, in order not to have to look at ourselves in the mirror." Over half a century before the invention of headphones, people were scared to take an honest look at themselves. The technology introduced since then has simply aided this human desire to hide from and distract ourselves.

If we were to relocate that husband's actions to other areas of life, they would probably seem a lot less strange. For instance, everyone on public transportation is plugged into their phones. Everyone you see running through a park has headphones in.

I'm barely exaggerating.

Everyone.

The problem with a nice dinner at a restaurant is that there is nothing you can do about the silences that insert themselves between topics. To this man (in my imagination), that dinner was the violent collision of his two worlds. The one he inhibits alone when he takes the L train and washes away the noise of the humanity around him with his music ran headfirst into his relationship with his woman. A relationship with a real person rather than prerecorded voices.

A relationship where sometimes silences fall.

I think so many of us become squirmy and uncomfortable in the midst of these silences, and this guy just couldn't handle it. It made me wonder, if he can't handle being quiet in the presence of his best friend, what does it look like when he is all alone? Is this man capable of existing outside of the noises and distractions, or has he reached the point where a even few seconds of solitude and silence is torturous?

We have become so accustomed to constantly being entertained that we have forgotten what it's like to be still. We'd rather be punched in the nards than endure an awkward silence.

I have learned that this preoccupation with noise can be outgrown if we make an effort. The past couple years I have forced myself into a habit of going for runs and leaving music behind. I love the sounds of birds singing and the breeze shaking the tree branches as it passes through. I like hearing the crunch of my rubber soles atop the gravel, dirt or pavement. Most of all, I leave music behind on the off chance I'll bump into someone willing to talk.

The sad thing is, most people don't want to talk. They don't want to hear the wildlife or the breeze. They don't even want to enjoy the stream of their own thoughts as their endorphins are released while they stride along the path. They're plugged in and consumed by whatever audio they're using to entertain themselves. Most people I see exercising can't survive an hour-long run without being plugged in! For me, it has become more of a relief to run *without* electronics and enjoy the temporary escape from noise. Give it a try, maybe you'll agree.

Dietrich Bonhoeffer also noted the dangers of clinging too closely to either extreme of introversion or extroversion:

> "Let him who cannot be alone beware of community... Let him who is not in community beware of being alone... Each by itself has profound perils and pitfalls. One who wants fellowship without solitude plunges into the void of words and feelings, and the one who seeks solitude without fellowship perishes in the abyss of vanity, self-infatuation and despair."

If we are so terrified of being alone, perhaps the best thing for us is not to avoid being alone, but rather, learn *how* to be alone.

Michael Cusick's *Surfing for God* has probably impacted my life more than any book I've ever read in regard to pornography addiction. In one chapter he talks about this inner noise and distraction and the lack of peace most of us experience.

> When we are alone, we encounter everything we have tried so hard to avoid. We face the emotional, relational, and spiritual noise that has been kept at bay by counterfeit good and counterfeit truth...it seems odd to say that we are averse to being with ourselves, much less with God. But we have become, as Kierkegaard said, tranquilized by the trivial. When the tranquilizer wears off and the analgesics of busyness and distraction lie beyond our reach, we have no other option but to face our inner worlds.
>
> In a recent conversation with my spiritual director, I asked why, even now, solitude can be so difficult for me. "When you are empty, being alone with yourself is almost always a scary thing," he said. "But when you are full, it is almost always a joy—like being with a good friend."

If you're at all like me, you've felt like a stranger in your own bones. You've felt the awkwardness of silence even when no one else is around and you can't escape into music or television. But hopefully you've also felt the opposite as well—that peace that comes with being alone and alright with it; you're at peace. When I say 'alone,' I mean away from music, podcasts, books or anything else we use to feel less alone, not simply away from other people.

Danny Malone's song *Weight on Me* became a familiar morose tune during my lonely first year of college. I remember many drives when it would play in the car and the last couple lines would hit me as hard as a meal at Waffle House. Not only were they wonderfully depressing, but they were incredibly relatable:

> The only way to find yourself
> is by yourself, by yourself.
> Well what if you're someone
> you don't really want to know?

I feel like a lot of us, especially those trapped in the perpetual grip of melancholy, wrestle with this feeling. *Sure, being alone with myself may be beneficial and healthy, but what if I don't even like myself?* I remember those thoughts well. In the years since those lonely drives around the bleak gray atmosphere of Cape Cod, I've learned to identify lies and separate them from truth.

Perhaps your parents didn't appreciate you the way they should have, or kids at school taught you to think you're a loser and an outcast. This is exactly why getting alone with the Lord is so vital to our spiritual health. How else will we rewire years of believing lies about ourselves that we're not good enough or that we're not really worth knowing unless we get alone with Him? I think that when we drown our lives with noise, we don't even really realize what we are believing. We can go on believing lies about ourselves for months or years without realizing it because we rarely take time to pause and sit in silence.

There is this story in 1 Kings 19 where Elijah realizes the same thing. If you're unfamiliar with some of the stories about Elijah, there is one point where he has a contest with a bunch of pagan priests on top of a mountain. The pagans called upon their gods to come and show up for hours, but nothing happens. Then Elijah calmly asks the real God to show up, and He does instantly, setting the mountaintop ablaze with fire. Elijah then has all the false priests slaughtered just because.

Immediately after Elijah has this mammoth victory against the pagan priests atop the mountain, you would think he'd be feeling pretty good, yah? Well, scripture says that the wicked queen Jezebel heard about what happened and was infuriated. She sent a messenger to Elijah to tell him she was going to come after him and kill him.

Now stop for a second and put yourself in Elijah's shoes.

You've just had the biggest victory of your life, to the extent that you killed 450 pagan priests. Yet you get spooked when a single woman threatens your life. (Granted, single women threaten my life constantly, but still.) Keep in mind that your victory on the mountain top was not because of your own physical strength, but because your God showed up and proved how powerful He is.

It's so easy to see some magnificent display of God's power, then turn around and return to that familiar place of fear. We should be at the peak of confidence, but our frail human natures and insecurities drive us to run and hide.

So Elijah takes off to a cave in the middle of nowhere. Not just a little off the beaten road, but forty days and forty nights of walking, and this is where we find him in chapter 19. An angel tells him that God is going to show up and speak to him, so he goes to the mouth of a cave to wait. And then it starts to get really interesting. (Because it wasn't before.)

While Elijah is standing there waiting for the Lord to show up, a huge wind rips through the valley and shatters rocks all around him. At this point, Elijah must have been thinking *Surely this is the Lord! He is about to show me something awesome!*

But God was not in the wind.

It doesn't say exactly who *was* in the big gust, but it was not the Lord. So Elijah keeps waiting. Soon, an earthquake comes and shakes the earth beneath his feet. Elijah probably began having the same thoughts again. A great and powerful force of nature has come again—surely it must be God this time.

But God was not in the earthquake either.

I wonder how confused Elijah was after seeing these two giant natural events one right after the other, only to realize that God wasn't in either of them. I would start to get suspicious. Because after the earthquake there was a huge fire.

But God was not in the fire.

Let's pause here and look at something. The first couple times I read this story, I breezed through the first three natural disasters and assumed it was dumb of Elijah to look for God in them. *Doesn't he know how God is* actually *going to appear in these things??* But then I realized that there are other points in the Bible where God *does* show up as those three very things—Wind, Earthquake and Fire.

Just not this time.

This time, after the fire passes, the Hebrew tells us that there was a "sound of silence." Many translations say that a *gentle whisper* came next. And Elijah doesn't only realize that God is in the silence; apparently there was something so powerful about this whisper that it caused Elijah to pull his cloak over his face before going to the opening of the cave.

Elijah was barely phased by the tornado, wildfire and earthquake, but when God appears in the silence, Elijah immediately covers his face.

I wonder how many times God has quietly spoken to me, but I was too busy drowning Him out with noise and distractions to hear.

I would wager that God often shows up in the silent times, but we are too busy or plugged in to hear Him. We may be obsessed with our jobs and busyness, or maybe it's just the constant stream of music flowing to our ears, but I think it's kind of obvious why most people I know claim that God never speaks to them like He did in the Bible.

We are foreign to stillness and quiet.

When I carve out time to spend with God, it's tempting to fill the silence with worship music or hymns. Because somehow that seems a lot more 'spiritual' than actual silence where God has room to speak and move. As good as worship music can be, maybe God wants to say something new and unique to us rather than the pre-recorded words on the latest Hillsong track. How will we know unless we unplug completely and spend time listening?

That's not to say He doesn't use the loud things like worship services, Christian conferences, and so on, but the silence is often where He speaks loudest. Just as Elijah was more prone to notice the wind and fire, we are often more prone to look to big happenings to find spiritual breakthroughs. But maybe we should spend more time looking to the quiet spaces between the events for God to speak.

"In a noise-polluted world," writes Susan Muto, "it is even difficult to hear ourselves think let alone try to be still and know God. Yet it seems essential for our spiritual life to seek some silence, no matter how busy we may be. Silence is not to be shunned as empty space, but to be befriended as fertile ground for intimacy with God."

In her book *Spiritual Disciplines Handbook*, Adele Ahlberg Calhoun dedicates an entire chapter to the discipline of silence. I contemplated copying and pasting the entire chapter here and just claiming it as my own, but I don't think the publishers would be very happy. So here are some of her paragraphs underscoring the importance of silence in the life of the faithful:

> "Silence challenges our cultural addiction to amusement, words, music, advertising, noise, alarms, and voices. Silence asks for patience and waiting. And both silence and waiting make us uncomfortable. They seem so unproductive. We can't tell if we are *doing* anything in them. So when we come upon silence, we fill it.
>
> We break the silence of travel with an iPod, the silence of the evening hours with the TV or computer, the silence of sleep with an alarm clock. Every part of our life is inundated with words—urgent words, random words, trivial words, hurtful words, managing words, religious words and on and on.
>
> Could it be that what we need is alone time with God and a lot fewer words? Do we need to push the "Do Not Disturb" button and learn what it is to be available to God alone?
>
> We need to realize that the world can go on without us for an hour or a day or even longer. The discipline of silence invites us to leave behind the competing demands of our outer world for time alone with Jesus. Silence offers a way of paying attention to the Spirit of God and what he brings to the surface of our souls.

If we want to find which spiritual practices to introduce to our own walk, we should look no further than to Jesus Himself. He was always retreating from the noisy crowds to be alone with His Father. Luke 5 tells us specifically that "Jesus often withdrew to lonely places and prayed." The kind of intimacy they experience there must be so rich because of how dedicated Jesus was to carving out time to be still before God.

In coming to understand this, I stumbled across a practice that has helped shape my walk with God more than any other spiritual discipline. Ironically, it is the lost art of learning to be still. I think a lot of us Christians in the West shy away from terms like 'meditation' and 'presence' because of odd New Age connotations, and this is a shame. Learning to see silence as a tool rather than the absence of *something* is something all Christians should use to their advantage. A friend introduced me to the ancient practice of Centering Prayer, and I want to share that with you, along with a few tips that helped me in my pursuit of silence.

Before I share the *how*, I want to explain a little bit more of the *why*.

This is a book about loneliness, so why am I encouraging you to get alone and spend time in silence? Shouldn't this book purely list useful ways to bridge the gap between you and those around you?

Well....

Understanding intimacy begins with an intimate knowledge of yourself. This is true in both our relationships with others and with God. In the next chapter, I'll talk more about why having a relationship with yourself is so important. Centering Prayer is a means to get to know yourself better. While 'solving' the issue of loneliness is done largely in community, there are elements of the struggle that require cultivating a peace with being alone.

The goal of Centering Prayer is to get to know yourself and God better simultaneously. The goal is not to accomplish anything or strive or achieve. The goal is to learn how to be still and accept doing nothing.

It's a practice of learning how to just *be*.

Sometimes as modern Western Christians, we hear phrases like *meditation* or *be present* and get spooked because of all the New Age associations. *We don't want to risk inviting satan into our hearts by meddling with this hippie mumbo jumbo.* Ironically, the practice of this silent, meditative, 'contemplative' prayer has roots which dig deep into Christian history. In his short book on Centering Prayer, J. David Muyskens records a brief overview of the history of contemplative prayer:

> In the Middle Ages it was expected that everyone could engage in contemplative prayer. Then in the late fifteenth and

early sixteenth centuries especially, many thought that only a few people could enjoy the gift of contemplative prayer. Common people were considered incapable of the practice. Most churches stopped teaching contemplative prayer to their members.

In the 1970s Eastern methods of meditation were attracting the interest of many young people in America. Three monks in Saint Joseph's Abbey in Spencer, Massachusetts, observed this phenomenon. They realized that this interest came out of hunger for a quiet and deep consciousness of the Ultimate Mystery. People were yearning for what the rich tradition of contemplative prayer in Christianity could provide, but most did not know about it. And the monks had no way to convey it like the carefully constructed methods of teaching developed for Eastern meditation such as Transcendental Meditation.

It's fascinating to me that the meditative practices people sought out in the 1970's—those practices most often associated with zen-type acid-dropping hippies—were really a return to this ancient Christian tradition. We all have a hunger to connect with God at the core of who we are, but this is impossible to achieve outside of silence and stillness.

Through the practice of Centering Prayer, Christians come to learn that God's love for them is not dependent on them performing or reaching a certain level of holiness (as if that were possible). The goal of Centering Prayer is to still our minds, calm our thoughts, and simply exist for a period of time. The name comes from the idea that at the core of the believer's personhood is the Holy Spirit, so intentionally engaging with silence is a way to return to our core, or, our center. Not only do we take steps toward the Holy Spirit since He resides at the center of who we are, but we get to know ourselves better. I know Ethan Renoe better as a result of being alone with him in silence, without distraction.

Prayer is a two-way conversation. When you have a conversation with a person, you (hopefully) do not speak the entire time. If you're doing it right, you should be speaking for about half the time and listening for half the time. The goal of Centering Prayer is to create space for God to speak to you, rather than you speaking to Him all the time. It's an exercise in listening.

Here's what I do: Choose a comfy chair and sit in a relaxed position. Be careful not to get so comfortable you drift off to sleep. I relax my arms and close my eyes, setting a timer for ten to twenty minutes. Then just sit in silence.

Silence from your computer, radio, and iPod.

Silence of your thoughts.

Silence in your heart.

Some people find it useful to choose a specific word to direct their daily Centering Prayer routine. For instance, perhaps your word of the day is 'Father.' As you sit in silence, your mind will begin to wander to errands you have to run, people you need to say something to, dogs you need to pet, and a myriad other things that will flood your mind. Use the word of the day to gently call yourself back to stillness and quiet. Return to thinking of God as a good Father who simply is enjoying sitting and spending time with you.

Perhaps your word of the day could be 'Present' and you focus on the nearness of God to you. There are endless possibilities! Make it personal. Create a habit that is special between you and God.

Again, Adele Ahlberg Calhoun provides some helpful insights to keep in mind while practicing Centering Prayer, especially when distractions or painful thoughts arise:

> In silence we often notice things we would rather not notice or feel. Pockets of sadness or anger or loneliness or impatience begin to surface. And as the silence settles in and nothing seems to be happening, we often struggle with the feeling that we are wasting time. As we remain in the silence though, the inner noise and chaos will begin to settle. Our capacity to open up wider and wider to God grows. The holy One has access to places

we don't even know exist in the midst of the hubbub.

As you quietly offer your body you can hone your listening reflexes. There is nothing you need to do here. This is not a time to come up with strategies to fix your life. Silence is a time to rest in God. Lean into God, trusting that being with Him in silence will loosen your rootedness in the world and plant you by streams of living water.

All of the spiritual disciplines are weird and awkward at first. Sometimes even painful. I have come to realize that most of them involve the removal of something, followed by patience. Fasting is the removal of food followed by counting down the hours until you can eat again. There is no way to 'speed-fast.' You can't stir up a few minutes of physical hunger and call it good.

In the same way, chastity is the removal of sexual activity from our lives until an appropriate time. You can't speed up the process (well, I guess there are ways...) but for the most part, the spiritual discipline of chastity also involves patience.

Just like the other practices, silence is a removal of distraction and noise for the sake of waiting upon the Lord. In silence, we invite Him to take a turn speaking. We quiet ourselves and our surroundings and offer that period of time up to Him. It is not a means to earn favor from Him, but a way to reorient ourselves and build the foundation of our days on peace.

I know I shouldn't make guarantees about things I can't promise, but in this one instance I will make an exception. If you commit to spending ten to twenty minutes a day in silence, you *will* notice a difference. Your mind and heart will feel less rushed and more at ease. You will find that for the rest of your day, you'll be more present and aware of the people and things around you. Silence reduces anxiety and stress. And the more you engage in the practice of Centering Prayer, the more natural it becomes.

I think developing comfort when we are alone with ourselves is one of the biggest obstacles to overcome in battling our loneliness. It probably sounds counter intuitive to get alone in order to combat our lonely feelings, but this is possibly the most effective step toward relief.

In learning to be still and silent when alone, we come to understand the difference between being *alone* and being *lonely*.

They do not have to be synonymous.

Give silence a shot. It will be weird and awkward at first. Silence will not happen on its own; we must be intentional about designating times and places to spend in silence, or it will never happen. Start small, just ten minutes a day. And watch as these few quiet minutes transform and bring peace to the rest of the day.

I wouldn't promise it if I didn't believe it.

Morning

I walked out of the bedroom and saw God seated at the kitchen counter reading the paper.

Crying.

We weren't talking.

Or at least I wasn't.

Nor was I listening.

KNOW YOURSELF

"I've always been me I guess I know myself"
-Drake

Recently I had to make a solo drive from Chicago to Denver. I have some friends in Kansas City, so I always break the trip in half there, enjoying the brutally delicious barbecue and admiring the Northern European architecture. And at some point on the leg from KC to Denver I had a breakthrough.

In the previous couple months, I had realized what a longwinded external processor I am. Through various conversations I had with friends as well as a brief examination of my past, I realized that I love to talk about what's going on in my life. And whenever I do that, I end up teaching myself some things I didn't know before. If you're like me, then you totally get it, and if you're an internal processor, just trust me. That's how it works for us.

One of the problems with being *such* an external processor is I feel bad when I have a massive data dump to unload on a friend and an hour or two passes before I even ask them how their day is going. So, more often than not, I give my friends the Cliff Notes version of my life details in order to spare them from becoming an audience to the monologue.

So as I drove from Kansas City, I realized I was tired of podcasts for the time being, mainly because there was a lot on my mind. Historically when that has happened, I would switch over to music for a time until I wanted to learn some more from podcasts. (I have been on a *lot* of road trips. I know the cycle: Serious podcasts such as sermons, switch to a funny one for relief, then finally music to let the brain relax and point its emotions at the passing views. Restart audio cycle.)

For the first time however, my millennial brain began craving something new: Silence mixed with intimacy. I think the internal dialogue went something like this:

> *Ethan: Well, I think I'm tired of these podcasts, even though they're so freaking good.*
>
> *Renoe: I know, that's weird. I don't even feel like any music at this point.*
>
> *Ethan: Does this mean we're old now?*
>
> *Renoe: Nah, I think it means something else. Mature maybe?*
>
> *Ethan: [Pretending to shoot windmills with fingers]*
>
> *Renoe: So…What should we listen to?*
>
> *Ethan: Well, we always wish there was someone riding with us, right? So we could talk to them?*
>
> *Renoe: Yah, but I've already called all the friends I can think of!*
>
> *Ethan: We could just ride in silence?*
>
> *[Both laugh]*

Ethan: Well, we could pray...

Renoe: Yah, but our brain always gets distracted when we pray and we lose our train of thought.

Ethan: We could pray out loud? Like God was sitting in the passenger seat?

Renoe: [Looks at the big black trash bag full of laundry in passenger seat.] I guess we could try it...It would be weird if anyone else heard us though.

Ethan: Who could possibly hear us?? The nearest living creatures are those cows getting funky on that hill over there!

Renoe: Wow. Weird.

Ethan: ...

Renoe: Okay, let's give it a shot.

The hardest part was starting.

It's weird to just start having a conversation with no one, even if no living soul on the planet will ever know. And I'm not talking about little mumbles under my breath like when you're doing chores around the house. I'm talking about a full on conversation, as if Jesus-in-the-flesh were buckled safely into the passenger seat. It took a few practice swings before I was able to launch into a full-fledged conversation, but once the words started flowing they didn't stop.

I told my Front Seat Friend about the people on my mind, the girls tugging at my heart, my fears about yet another move (the third of the year), and my excitement about coming connections. I probably told Him a lot about my episodes of loneliness, struggles with lust, and how I want to be a more patient man.

As I poured out my heart to the trash bag in the front seat, the conversation progressively got deeper. Perhaps I finally came to believe it wouldn't judge me for exposing my soul. I began telling it about areas in which I felt weak, where my identity had been compromised. In saying a lot of these things out loud, I realized they were not really me. As certain lines came out of my lips, I realized I had subconsciously been believing a handful of these lies without even examining where they came from.

As I continued speaking and identifying a lot of these lies, truths began to come out—things I used to know about myself, like my pioneering spirit and leadership abilities. The fact that, for some kooky reason, people tend to listen when I speak, and follow when I do things.

I have no idea how long I talked to my new best friend The Trash Bag, but I remember being all talked-out and then the two of us just sat there in silence. Eventually I switched a podcast back on, but opening up *about* myself *to* myself was one of the most healing times of my life. I felt relieved and rested, like I had woken up from a solid nap. Fear was reduced and my identity was restored.

While I was driving and talking to myself, I learned a couple things. First, if you can't find anyone to talk to, talk to God/yourself. I had a mentor a few years ago named Ethan who used to tell me that being honest with the Lord is nearly the same as being honest with yourself (And no, this time it wasn't me talking to myself. His name was actually Ethan).

I realized there are pieces of myself I don't like to look at or think about, so being able to bring them up before myself *and* before God was incredibly helpful and healing. In the years since Ethan (the other one) first told me that, I've proven over and over again how true it is. When I can admit things about myself *to* myself, it's easier to admit them to God and hand them to Him, trusting Him with them.

The second thing I learned is that talking to God is just as beneficial as talking to another human for an external processor like me. Don't get me wrong—I love talking to people. A lot. But there is something freeing about buckling Jesus into the front seat and unloading all your thoughts onto Him. He is the only one who won't grow tired of hearing you talk or get exhausted from walking with you through the darker areas of you. I discovered how freeing it was to speak without limit or boundary, but to just express myself however I pleased and know that someone was listening who cared about every intricate detail.

There are so many benefits in releasing your thoughts and feelings, and sometimes the only ones there to hear you are God and yourself. So give it a shot. Talk to yourself. Talk to God. You'll probably come to see that getting things out in front of you help to also get them out before the Lord, and by deepening your intimacy with Him, you'll begin to take steps away from loneliness.

When someone doesn't know himself, there's a good chance he doesn't let other people get to know him either. I think this is true of all of us at various points in our lives. My friend Michael John Cusick has pointed out that the word *integrity* comes from the same root as the word *integer*, meaning 'whole'. Someone who has integrity is a whole person. They are the same person over here with *this* group of friends as they are over there with *that* group of friends.

Someone who is not whole is more wishy-washy. They may be the clown in one gang, but the philosopher in another. And over here, they play the role of the athlete. I catch myself doing this all the time. My identity can be dependent on the people I'm around. When I hang out with intensely intelligent theologians, I become the 'dumb funny guy.' But put me in a group of college students who want to know more about God and suddenly I'm the sage who only thinks holy thoughts and regularly spills wisdom from the scriptures.

I love the way Dan Allender described this routine in an interview one time. He said that people today tend to be very broken hearted. "Not broken hearted as in sad or full of grief; instead, we are broken into fragmented selves that are unable to do much other than posture and pretend we are someone whom we know we are not. This deep inner schism enables us to function as one self with our spouse and an hour later to lurk on a site where seduction and role-playing allows us to escape to another fantasized self." He was talking about porn addiction toward the end, but the same is true in our social groups. We can pretend to be a collection of people living inside one body, depending on who is around us.

In his legendary *Confessions,* Saint Augustine refers to this as "my disintegrated self." He says that when his desires were diverse and he "pursued a multitude of things, I went to pieces."

I've come to find that people who know themselves well can transition easily from funny to deep conversation. They're not scared of talking about deep things, yet they don't feel like they always have to hide behind their intelligence. Maybe you're someone who uses humor to hide your real self, and you tend to shy away from deeper discussions. Whatever the case, our goal should be to become people who know ourselves well enough to be the same person no matter who we're with, the truest version of ourself. When we come to know ourselves well, we don't need to hide behind wit, fashion, money, intelligence, or whatever it is we show the world to try to convince it that we're valuable.

My favorite people to hang out with are those who are comfortable being themselves rather than acting like someone they're not.

The best test to determine if you are guilty of this is to think about your various friend groups. Throw your parents, siblings and cousins in there too. Would it be a good idea for them all to converge and hang out together? Or would it be awkward for you because you'd suddenly have to play different roles simultaneously? Most of the time we develop these characters simply because it fits well with that specific group of friends or family.

Don't let the people around you determine your identity. My guess is, they did not force you to play a certain role; we tend to do that to ourselves. We get it in our heads that *these* people will like us more if we were like *this,* so we modify ourselves to fit the part. The best way to become the same person 24/7 is to intentionally spend time alone. Get to know yourself in silence as I mentioned in the last chapter. Write or talk to yourself. Become a whole person of integrity rather than a fragmented, shape-shifting person.

When intense feelings of loneliness arise, it can be discouraging. It feels like there is nothing we can do about it; there is no elixir to suddenly make us feel more whole.

In the heat of the moment, there are two options: Embrace it or escape it.

To escape it means to flip on a screen of some sort and put your mind at ease, engaging with fictitious characters who will be supplemental friends for 22 minutes. Or perhaps your device of choice is to exercise until the pain is gone, running mile after painful mile, far beyond the healthy limit. Maybe it's a new boyfriend or just a one-night stand. For others of us, our escape of choice is work disguised as healthy productivity. One thing I've noticed about coping mechanisms, or whatever you want to call them, is that most of them are not that bad by themselves. But when they are elevated to the position of an anesthesia for our pain, or when we use them in excess, they attempt to heal a wound they cannot.

They are unable to bear the weight of our loneliness.

Choosing to embrace rather than escape our suffering is almost unfathomable in the moment of loneliness.

The hardest thing about this is the patience necessary for it to be productive. Most of the time it just feels like waiting and seeing nothing happen. In the rare times I am able to choose embrace over escape, I find myself journaling or praying. The past few years, I've started journaling my prayers like letters.

I'll let you peek under the envelope.

When I was in high school, I read the book *Cry, The Beloved Country* which is about a pastor in segregated South Africa. All of his townsfolk call him *Umfundisi*, the Zulu word for 'pastor'. Since my father is a pastor, I began calling him Umfundisi, and the name stuck. I love it because it is unique to us. No other American kid calls their dad *Umfundisi*, so it's a special connection between us. When he hears that unique African name, he knows that his son—and only his son—is talking to him. In the same way, I don't call anyone else *Umfundisi* because they would look at me like I just ate a whole tube of toothpaste.

In the same way, I have a secret name for God—a nickname of sorts—to whom I address each letter/prayer/journal entry. I'm not going to reveal it here, but it also has African roots and reflects a unique and quirky aspect of my relationship with Him. I wonder if part of our difficulty in reconciling God and our loneliness is that we see Him as an ethereal spirit or an energy rather than a Person. We have a Star Wars mentality in which The Force is all around us and in everything, and if we work really hard, we can harness its power. But when we see God through this Star Wars mindset, there is no relating to Him. You can't have a relationship with The Force, you can only study it and use it.

The Force is mysterious, unlike God, who has made Himself known through Christ and in Scripture. God is a person. If He weren't, how could we possibly have relationship with Him?

I address God and then, as vulnerably as I can, pour out what is on my mind that night (It seems to happen the most at night. I guess every morning is pregnant with so much possibility I don't think to be lonely until the day has evaporated).

If you thought my published writing was raw and vulnerable, you can only imagine what my private journal is like. The more open and vulnerable you can be with the Lord, the better. Writing out my journals letter-style helps me open up and bring pieces of myself to the Lord that I couldn't do simply thinking by myself. Perhaps it's because I'm an extrovert or an external processor or both, but this has proven to be a practical aid in times of deep despair when a road trip with Trash Bag is not immediately available.

One thing to note about self-examination and emotional registry though, is that it is tiring. The reason we don't jump up and down at the idea of writing out our feelings, or even going to a counselor for that matter, is it's tiring. It's painful work. It is not an easy task to sit and write out your guts to the Lord.

I was on the phone with a friend a few months ago as he told me about the counseling he's been going through over the summer. He explained that it was so good and so healthy for him, but it was hard work. I asked him what he meant by *hard work*, and he explained that drawing up all these old emotions and memories like oil rigs pulling fuel up to the surface was taxing. Not only was it emotionally tiring to revisit places in his past, but it was physically tiring at times. Using all that brain power to think through and analyze old times can really take a toll.

On top of the weariness, processing old, or even current emotions is time consuming. Who wouldn't rather go out with friends and dance the loneliness away than sit in silence for an hour with a pen and paper, or a counselor, digging below the surface?

I wonder if part of this distance we often feel from God is a fear of stepping on His divine toes. We're worried we may offend Him with our thoughts or our anger. We filter our words so they can fit better into the mold of "good, Christian language." I can't tell you how many times I've heard phrases like *Dude, you can't say that in here! It's a church!*

I think the Bible has a much different idea for our employment of language.

This is why the Psalms are so great: The word in the Bible which we read as "heart" usually means "guts" in Hebrew. It's the deepest part of who you are. It's the thing that rises when you fall off a bridge, or in love. You may tell God what's on your mind. You may even share with Him some emotions you are weathering. But you haven't poured out your guts.

Even Jesus seemed unafraid of being judged for His words before God.

He wasn't scared of pouring His guts out to God.

In the most intense moment of His life, hours before His painful death, Jesus is in the Garden of Gethsemane, wailing before His Father, sweating blood and begging for God to spare His life.

Take this cup from me,

He cried.

Jesus straight up told God that He doesn't want to do the very thing God had told Him to do.

There was a professor at my college who always declared in his thick Bostonian accent, "Saints! You shouldn't sweah. But if you're going to sweah, sweah when you pray. I cuss all the time before the Lawd!"

If any of you are like me, there is a cognitive block somewhere in your soul that tells you, "these words are okay, but these over here...are not." There's something that tells me that too much honesty is sinful.

I am trying to undo this.

I think this barrier of politically polite language has actually built a wall between the Lord and I rather than enhanced our relationship. It's like I've been trying to paint a sunset without any red paint. You'll get the general idea, but the force of the fiery clouds will lose their vigor.

Language is important because it is the means through which we perceive, interpret, and communicate reality, communicate life. So in a sense, limiting your language before God limits the extent to which you can live before Him. We tend not to filter ourselves with our closest friends and family, yet we do it before God who already knows our thoughts and actions.

Earlier today I was trying to explain what Systematic Theology is to a friend, and as the words exited my mouth, they felt so small and limp. I was explaining that it's about creating a system in which the aspects of our faith—salvation, Christology, ecclesiology, soteriology, et cetera—all work together to form a unified, functioning machine. It's about creating a simple, well-oiled system that makes sense to us and is easily digestible.

What I'm realizing though is that God is not a system.

He does not come gift wrapped in a cute little box with blue and red ribbons.

The moment you've got Him pegged as a pillar of fire, He reappears somewhere else as a whisper. You start thinking He is a lamb and suddenly He rips out some organs as a hungry lion.

"Safe?" C.S. Lewis once wrote about the Lord. "Who said anything about safe? 'Course he isn't safe. But He's good."

I fear that my conception of God has become far too small. I find myself hiding things from Him (as if He didn't already see and know them) because I'm worried about intruding upon His sensibilities. Let us pour out our guts before Him and demolish the walls in which we have placed Him.

Try journaling or talking to Him without a filter. I think that by developing a more open and honest language before the Lord, we will begin to experience deeper intimacy with Him, and in this, crawl further away from those feelings of loneliness and isolation.

Many of us are lonely because we do not know ourselves. We look in the mirror and see only an image of someone we'd like to be. Someone we're striving to be.

The only route to knowing ourselves better—more authentically—is through brutal honesty. There is no shortcut that circumvents honesty, vulnerability, and typically, pain. Looking into the mirror of our souls is difficult and our tendency is to look away in favor of imagining some stronger or cooler version of ourselves.

I think that knowing yourself is not a matter of being able to describe yourself accurately, or knowing a lot of facts about yourself.

"Ethan is x, y, and z."

We all already know the facts about ourselves. I think it's a matter of being able to be still with ourselves; alone with ourselves in a way that is peaceful. It's the ability to know all of our flaws and still be alright with them in a quiet room. When you can sit with them without needing to escape them into noise, distraction, relationships, parties, porn, drugs, or whatever your release of choice is. Knowing ourselves is the art of coming to peace with who we are, without having to cover up.

We must realize that we can be accepted just as we are.

We need to learn the art of openness. Of talking to the trash bag in the front seat in order to become more familiar with our own thoughts and struggles. And as we come to be more honest with ourselves, we will come to be more open with God. He is not offended by our anger or our despair. He is not afraid of what will come out of our mouths, but I think we are.

If you're tired of hiding behind different versions of yourself, try getting to know yourself. The real you. The one you weren't scared to be when you were a little kid. The real you may be less cool or a little weaker, or a little less intelligent than you act, but he will be real. The real you is tired of pretense and prefers honesty.

So get to know yourself. I bet you'll appreciate what you find.

5/26/14

We humans are such fragile things
it hardly takes a touch
to tear apart a self we made
and throw it in the dust.
We walk around inside of shells,
our exoskeletons.
And should it break or chip away,
our instinct is to run.
I bought a fancy painted one
from someone we both know.
Its colors were so loud this shield
was quite hard to ignore.
But lo it broke and fell apart
and naked did I stand
without a friend to sit by me
or come and hold my hand.
But in the stillness came a sound
so quiet and so soft.
He asked why I had tried to hide
and run from Him so oft.
Before my lips could even move
or answer fill my mind,
He picked me up and dressed me in
an effervescent shine.
Its beauty never faded and
it wouldn't hide me well,
because it showed me me me me
and wrenched me from my cell.
I enter in the wedding feast
and never have to be
a wanderer from out the fold
of God eternally.
His gentle hands have gathered all
the pieces of my shell
and rendered them quite useless by
deliv'ring them to hell.

JESUS WON'T TAKE AWAY YOUR LONELINESS

"But Jesus often withdrew to lonely places and prayed."
-Luke 5:16

In 1962, John Glenn was preparing to be the third man shot into space. They were devout Christians who wanted only to please the Lord, so before his launch date, he and his wife Annie paid regular visits to their pastor in Ohio to make sure there was nothing in the Bible that would forbid his departure. After a number of meetings and months of scouring the scriptures, the Glenns and their pastor were convinced there was nothing inherently sinful about going to space, so John moved forward with his mission.

On February 20, Glenn boarded his ship, the Friendship 7, and left the atmosphere. While he was orbiting the earth, somewhere over Southeast Asia he began to notice small golden glowing orbs. "They look like little stars or fireflies" he reported through the communications radio. "There are literally thousands of them."

He was outside the ship and floating weightless through a field of small glimmering globes, thinking that somehow, God was reaching out to him or trying to communicate something grand.

Upon his return, news spread about John Glenn orbiting the earth and coming back having seen a miracle from God. He claimed that the only possible explanation for the glowing balls was the Divine reaching out to touch him and show humanity something spectacular. America was captivated by these mysterious glowing orbs of outer space.

It did not take long for the mystery to be solved, however. Later that year, astronaut Scott Carpenter boarded the Aurora 7 and discovered the source of the thousands of glowing spheres.

They were pee.

As the ship had orbited the earth and flushed the waste from the cabin, the astronauts' urine had frozen into thousands of tiny golden orbs, illuminated as the sun hit them.

No doubt the vision of these orbs *was* heavenly and certainly would have seemed like an act of God to the generation that initiated trips into space, but the explanation for them seems like somewhat of a letdown. Of course, God did create the sun and gravity and the vacuum of outer space, and even pee, but the scientific explanation leaves us somewhat wanting. We want to read about divine encounters and miraculous occurrences rather than having them explained away by science-minded post-Enlightenment scrooges.

Even more regular occurrences can stir us to awe and wonder if we let them: A thunder and lightning storm are much more than positively and negatively charged ion clouds. A sunset is not simply atmospheric chemicals fragmenting light rays into certain wave spectrums. Even life itself, as we watch a flower or a tree grow, is much more than a mere scientific reaction.

These things are simultaneously divine and natural. They are marvels from God, but they also have natural and logical explanations.

I think the same is true of our loneliness.

Many Christians have this tendency to 'over-spiritualize' things, assuming they can plug God into the equation and everything will be solved. I can't roll my eyes high enough when I hear phrases like,

Oh, you're lonely? Just give it to God.

or,

Christians shouldn't feel lonely...God is always with them!

Where in the Bible is this magical verse? I realize this may seem antithetical to THE PREVIOUS CHAPTER ON JESUS DWELLING WITH US IN OUR LONELINESS, and to some degree, yes, these chapters are meant to compliment one another. Recognizing that Jesus has entered into our fallen flesh should give us hope that He knows what it is to suffer, to be alone and rejected. And we take this knowledge into our time alone with Him and let it inform our relationship with Him.

But solving the issue of loneliness can't be done entirely alone. It requires *human* community. I would go so far as to say that to some extent,

Jesus can't fix your loneliness.

I think we often do what John Glenn did when he was orbiting the world: We over-spiritualize things in our lives which should be seen as natural and explainable. Just like he thought the frozen tinkle was a sign from God, many of us are waiting for a miracle to happen and zap away our loneliness when the solution is really more natural than that.

Yesterday I went to a Christian high school here in Colorado and spent the day conducting surveys with the students, asking questions about their experiences with loneliness. One of the questions I asked was, *When you feel lonely, how do you think God interacts with your loneliness? Does He? Or are God and your loneliness completely separate in your mind?*

The answers from the students were very telling. One 8th grade boy very honestly (and eloquently) reported, "No, not really. I feel like he isn't there. I haven't heard him, like ever."

Another girl in seventh grade wrote, "Sometimes when I feel lonely, I feel a little mad at God because I know He's there but it doesn't seem to fix the pain."

And one senior answered, "There was a time when I asked my worship pastor what to do when I was lonely. She said 'lean on God.' I didn't know how to, so I didn't do anything. I don't really feel like He's there."

In fact, I added up all the answers and out of 146 students, only 25 reported ever thinking about God interacting with their loneliness. That's about 83% who have *never* experienced Him in their lonely hours. Most of the students wrote that they had never thought about the two correlating, and that they mostly receive only silence from God when they reached out to Him.

Perhaps God is *not* sufficient to drive out all our lonely feelings. And maybe we shouldn't expect Him to be.

Look at Genesis 2, after God created man in the Garden of Eden. Adam was all alone in the garden, despite being surrounded by animals. He had a duty to name all the animals and take care of them. He also had all the food, water, and tiger-wrestling he could hope for. He also had something else that was totally unique to this period in time.

He had perfect relationship with God.

Genesis 3 tells us God would come down "in the cool of the afternoon" and walk with Adam. In other words, there was no separation between God and man, and God would just come down to earth and kick it. Everything was still perfect. Adam had all the access to God he could possibly ask for. There was no barrier between him and the Lord. This was *before* the fall of man; it was before the fruit was eaten.

Everything was perfect, and God had just finished declaring everything in the universe *good*.

Everything, that is, save one.

There was one thing God sees after a while and says it's *not* good. The Lord looked down and saw that the man was all alone and said, "It is *not good* for man to be alone." In spite of his perfect relationship with God, Adam was still *alone*.

Put another way, God was not enough to satiate Adam's loneliness.

When we offer overly spiritual advice to friends and family who are suffering or even just going through a lonesome season, we may not be addressing the issue properly. When a single mother is struggling to provide for her kids, reciting pithy spiritual quotes at her won't put food in their tummies, food will. Taking time to cook for them and deliver a meal will. Quasi-biblical Jesus-jargon won't.

Even Jesus knew this to be true, which is why He always addressed people's physical issues and ailments before teaching them spiritual truths. When people came to Jesus asking for healing and miracles, He met them where they were, rather than simply saying, "God is with you, chill."

When it comes to us addressing our loneliness, I think the same is true. Abstract uplifting maxims don't do the work necessary to alleviate us of our pain. While I absolutely believe God can lift our burdens and carry them for us, there are often more natural and practical measures we can take. For instance, we can cry out to God about our loneliness day after day, or we can get out and join clubs, groups, sports leagues, etc in order to fix the problem.

Dietrich Bonhoeffer has a unique way of uniting these two relationships —our relationship with others and our relationship with God—and would argue that in creating Christian community, we are in fact communing with God. If you have been in church for any amount of time, you have probably heard the phrase "The Body of Christ" thrown around, and may not have ever given it much thought. What does it mean that we, Christians, are Jesus' body?

It means when we extend love to another person, we are tangibly becoming Jesus to them. When we hug someone, it is as if Jesus were hugging them, because we are the physical bodies of Christ in the world. Since Jesus is no longer physically on this earth, we have the opportunity to be Christ to each other. When we take a meal to a widow, we are acting as the tangible Body of Christ; we are physically acting out a spiritual reality.

Do you feel distant from God? Engage with your Christian community and be intentional about experimenting with what it means to be Christ to one another. One central element of tangibly acting out what it means to be Jesus with skin on may catch some of us by surprise: Confession of sin. Bonhoeffer writes,

> "Christ became our Brother in order to help us. Through him our brother and sister has become Christ for us in the power and authority of the commission Christ has given him. Our brother stands before us the sign of the truth and the grace of God. He has been given to us to help us. He hears the confession of our sins in Christ's stead and he forgives our sins in Christ's name. He keeps the secret of our confession as God keeps it. When I go to my brother to confess, I am going to God."

Bonhoeffer also writes extensively about the value of praying for and with our brothers and sisters. These things may seem like simplistic and natural actions, but in reality, when we think of one another as the actual Body of Christ coming to us in physical form, we unite our spirituality and our community. God is no longer an abstract concept, but comes to us in the form of our family and friends.

Just as in communion, where the body and blood of Jesus take on the appearance of bread and wine, we have the opportunity to physically reach out and show love to others around us. Sometimes, our tendency is to think about God *over here* and our friends and community *over there*. What the Bible shows us is, when the Holy Spirit lives inside someone, that individual has the opportunity to go and be Jesus to another human, as if Jesus Himself were in the room. When we pray for someone, when we give to someone, when we confess our sins together, we are embodying God to one another. Our spirituality and our physical existence live much closer together than we think, and we are remiss to divorce them.

Rather than telling you that *God is there for you, just go spend time with Him,* I want us to come to a fresh understanding of community. Perhaps one of the best ways to experience God is to gather with others and pray. Sing hymns. Read scripture together. And in doing so, we bring one another closer to intimacy with God and away from loneliness.

Hebrews 13 echoes this exhortation when it says, "Do not stop meeting together, as some are in the habit of doing." When we fail to come together as the Body of Christ, we not only grow farther apart from one another, but from God. If we truly are "Little Christs,"—which is what the word *Christian* means—we should take every opportunity to connect one another to God; to be Christ with skin on to each other.

Our relationship with God is not always invisible and abstract. Sometimes it looks like the people in your life encouraging you or bringing you hot chocolate.

When it comes to eliminating loneliness from our lives, sometimes the solution is far more practical and common sense than we may think. I realize I'm as extroverted as they come, so telling you to simply go out and meet people may seem daunting. But humans weren't made to exist in a vacuum, even the most introverted among us.

The author Donald Miller, a self-proclaimed introvert and recluse, even realized the value in creating relationships and spending time with other people. He sums up the practicality of human community as an alternative to loneliness:

> Loneliness is something that happens to us, but I think it is something we can move ourselves out of. I think a person who is lonely should dig into a community, give himself to a community, humble himself before his friends, initiate community, teach people to care for each other, love each other. Jesus does not want us floating through space or sitting in front of our televisions. Jesus wants us interacting, eating together, laughing together, praying together.

Jesus won't always take away your loneliness.

Sometimes it takes other people—ones with skin that you can touch and hug—to alleviate the ache in our bones. And not just one, but a community. A church. Imagine if churches were seen as welcoming destinations for the lonely. If they were places where people could walk in and be welcomed; all the congregants would gather around and bandage one another's wounds.

We were made for community, so often, escaping our loneliness means simply not being alone.

1/2/16

Once more,
let me inquire of the Lord,
for O! is His silence jarring to my senses.
Ten times ten times ten times
did I call out to Him from the place of my sin.
And every time His answer was the same:
[*silence*]

Yet even more times has His mercy reached my
knees, rising until I drowned in it.
Even more times has He picked me up from my filth,
naked and spent,
unable to hide and too frail to run.

I've run from You,
O Keeper of my salvation.

O, how I have departed!

I have longed for Your death, that I
may take my inheritance now,
impatient son that I am.

But ten times ten times ten times
have you sought me out in the valley of the dead,
taking me from my place of sin
to Your hill of resurrection.

CONCLUSION

So.

You've reached the conclusion of the book and you're still lonely. You still have a gnawing pain in your ribs which threatens to eat the life right out of you some days. You may have picked up this book looking for answers or a formula or a magic salve to rub on your lonely achey parts. But nope. This is all you've got.

I've said it once and I'll say it again: Books won't heal your loneliness. TV shows won't heal your loneliness.

Humans will.

Vulnerability and intimacy will.

Eye contact will.

Time will.

And God will.

Building a community and changing our cyclical habits which lead us back into loneliness take a lot of time. It may be foreign to you to enter a space and not instantly try to fill it with music, or to encounter a quiet room and not reach for your phone.

Don't be distracted. Focus here.

We are the New Lonely, and we are way too far away. We are removed from the present moment and the present space where we are. Be careful not to mistake your lack of peace for loneliness. Chances are, you are more connected than most people throughout human history. The issue isn't a lack of people, it's a lack of intimacy and peace.

If we have any hope of recovering intimacy with ourselves, much less with God, we must relearn the ancient art of being still. If you feel far away from yourself, or are constantly hiding behind clothes, fashion trends, humor, or thousands of other defense mechanisms, it's likely because you have not spent much time with yourself.

I always recognize when I am unaware of myself. I feel more empty and rush to fill the silent void with a podcast or magazine. We are called human *beings*, yet we need to learn how to just *be*. We're always busy trying to impress God with all of our good works or devoted prayer lives. We're constantly trying to win the affections of others with our cool haircuts or witty tweets. Where we fail is recognizing that we have value simply by *being*.

This is why Henri Nouwen points out the delicious joy in celebrating our birthdays.

> Birthdays need to be celebrated. I think it is more important to celebrate a birthday than a successful exam, a promotion, or a victory. Because to celebrate a birthday means to say to someone: 'thank you for being you.' Celebrating a birthday is exalting life and being glad for it. On a birthday we do not say: 'thanks for what you did, or said, nor accomplished.' No, we say: 'Thanks you for being born and being among us.'
>
> On birthdays we celebrate the present. We do not complain about

what happened or speculate about what will happen, but we lift someone up and let everyone say, 'We love you.'

Celebrating a birthday reminds us of the goodness of life, and in this spirit we really need to celebrate people's birthdays every day, by showing gratitude, kindness, forgiveness, gentleness, and affection. These are ways of saying: 'It's good that you are alive; it's good that you are walking with me on this earth. Let's be glad and rejoice..."

Thanks for *being*.

When we return to this simple truth, that we are loved as we are, simply because we exist, not because we *do* anything, it helps us return to a place of peace rather than a hasty feeling of unrest and a need to impress.

Let us learn once more the art of *being*, and nothing more.

The New Lonely is not just a group of misfits or nerds. It not the awkward kid in the corner who always talks about aliens, or the grandma who whittles away her days knitting in her rocker.

The New Lonely is you and me.

It's our neighbors and classmates. It's the people on Facebook you envy the most, as well as the ones you feel sorry for.

It's the high schooler I had dinner with tonight who told me about a school program he went on this year. It was called Senior Solo, and the teachers blindfolded the students and drove them into the mountains, dropping them off all alone in the wilderness. They were only allowed a notebook and Bible, and were given some writing prompts for journaling.

He told me he blasted through the prompts just to distract his mind from the stillness of nature, but once they were exhausted, he simply sat there.

He said it took him at least an hour to convince himself that it was okay to just be still and enjoy doing nothing while sitting in the mountains.

That little irritation in his brain that prevented him from being still is the New Loneliness.

It's hard to pinpoint and harder to escape.

The New Lonely is not a death sentence though. We are not beyond hope and bound to our loneliness like a tattoo. After all, we are human beings. We are a people who are dynamic and changing. We are learning and growing and building relationships and having our hearts broken.

The New Lonely are not beyond repair.

We are resilient and eager.

When we find ourselves in dark times and the weather radar inside of us shows storms in the forecast, we can now be aware of a few of the roots. We can recognize the absence of stillness in our lives and an abundance of distraction contributing to our lachrymose moods.

Let's build more bridges and burn fewer. Connect yourself to those around you, and not by sending a friend request. Get coffee with someone and ask them the hard questions. Strive for intimacy at all costs. Delete everything that prevents this, even if that means certain *social* media.

We are the New Lonely, but not forever.

We're all alone.

Let's be alone together.

e

ETHAN

Ethan has lived on six continents and more than half of the United States of America. He attended three colleges and recently graduated from Moody Bible Institute in Chicago with a B.A. in Communications. Thanks to a chance media encounter while on a run in downtown Chicago in December 2015, Ethan became a viral sensation with over 5 million hits and features on national networks and international television. When he isn't co-founding non-profits in Nigeria or backpacking across Brasil, he can usually be found writing at a downtown coffee shop or helping clients achieve their personal fitness goals. But his favorite job of them all is being a youth pastor to a bunch of nerds in Colorado. A frequent speaker and conference leader, Ethan blogs regularly at ethanrenoe.com.

Made in the USA
San Bernardino, CA
11 April 2018